The Loving Search for God

Contemplative Prayer
and *The Cloud of Unknowing*

The Loving Search for God

- Contemplative Prayer
and *The Cloud of Unknowing*

William A. Meninger, O.C.S.O.

Foreword by
THEOPHANE THE MONK

B L O O M S B U R Y
LONDON · OXFORD · NEW YORK · NEW DELHI · SYDNEY

A Continuum Book
Bloomsbury Publishing Plc
50 Bedford Square
London WC1B 3DP

www.bloomsbury.com

Bloomsbury Publishing, London, New Delhi, New York and Sydney

First published 1997

A CIP record for this book is available from the British Library

ISBN 978 0 8264 0851 8

10 9 8 7 6 5

Library of Congress Cataloging-in-Publication Data
Meninger, William.
The loving search for God : contemplative prayer and the
cloud of unknowing / William A. Meninger.
p. cm.
ISBN 0-8264-0682-3 (hdb. : alk. paper)
ISBN 0-8264-0851-6 (pbk.)
1. Cloud of unknowing. 2. Mysticism—Catholic Church.
3. Contemplation. 4. Spiritual life—Catholic Church.
5. Catholic Church—Doctrines. I. Title.
BV5080.C6M46 1994
248.2'2—dc20 94-21313
CIP

Printed and bound in the United States of America

This little book
is dedicated to everyone,
past and present,
who has accompanied me
in the loving search.
I would like to
single out especially
my sister, Helen, and the
monks of my community.

Scripture passages
are taken from the
Revised Standard Version
and the New
International Version.

· Contents

· Foreword

William is a beautiful person. He says this is an utterly simple book. It comes from his own experience, and he speaks from the heart.

A parish priest for six years, he entered the Trappist Community in Spencer, Massachusetts, whose abbot was Dom Thomas Keating. The simplification in his own prayer life puzzled him at first. Then he picked up the little fourteenth-century classic *The Cloud of Unknowing*. Here he found confirmation and clarification. It became for him a vade mecum. Assigned to conduct retreats for the parish priests who came to the monastery, he found that he was able to speak to them convincingly of this simple, simple way of prayer.

That was twenty-five years ago. Now, having reread *The Cloud* more than a hundred times, and taught this simple method to thousands, and practiced what he preached, he sets his hand to writing this "utterly simple book." Good. Read it.

William's experience in teaching this prompted another beautiful person at Spencer, Basil, to begin teaching the same method. You've heard of Basil Pennington. So many books—*Daily We Touch Him, Centering Prayer, Centered Living, Call to the Center, The Way Back Home, Awake in the Spirit.* . . . So many trips—China, India, Africa, Australia. Boundless energy, immense heart.

Abbot Thomas Keating retired in 1981 and followed William to Spencer's Daughter House, St. Benedict's Monastery, in Snowmass, Colorado. Here he became convinced of a widespread thirst in laypeople for this kind of thing. He experimented with a two-week intensive retreat, with five hours of centering prayer (as it was now called) each day. Soon the contemplative outreach was underway, now with introductory workshops, retreats, advanced retreats, teachers, and coordinators throughout the country as well as support groups. Books followed—*Open Mind–Open Heart, The Mystery of Christ, Invitation to Love, Intimacy with God*. All this from one centered monk.

I am happy to recommend these three beautiful persons to you. The same central teaching, but each with different temperament and gifts. They share a common monastic experience, but William had his years in the parish, and, a scripture scholar, he was enriched by three years in the Holy Land. Basil was a theologian at Vatican II, and has done considerable research in the early monastic tradition. Thomas had the dreadful pastoral experience of being abbot through the sixties and seventies, and has been concerned to work out a description of the entire "spiritual journey" that can be appreciated by ordinary folk in our time. My impression has been that all three practice what they preach.

May they lead you into the heart of God.

THEOPHANE THE MONK
St. Benedict's Monastery
Snowmass, Colorado

· Introduction

Dear Friend in God,

For over twenty-five years I have been giving retreats and workshops on contemplative prayer as taught by a fourteenth-century book called *The Cloud of Unknowing* by an unknown English author. Inspired myself by the loving union with God that *The Cloud* teaches, I have been blessed with the privilege of teaching it to thousands of others. I have read *The Cloud* over a hundred times, and each time I find it a new book, a new inspiration, a source of new ideas about the "work of love" (the descriptive phrase *The Cloud* uses to describe contemplative prayer!) or "the loving search," as I call it herein.

It will not be surprising then to tell you that I have recommended the book over and over again to those whom I have taught. I have been delighted by their response when I have had the opportunity to read and comment on chapters of *The Cloud* and then to learn how often they obtain the book so that they can read it slowly and repeatedly as I suggest to them. However, I must tell you, dear friend, that I have been very often disappointed upon learning that when they read *The Cloud* on their own, they find it very difficult, at times impossible, to understand. This is true even of priests, nuns, and well educated lay people. The reason is, of course, that *The Cloud* was written from and for a fourteenth-century culture. Some of the ideas and many of the methods of communicating them are unfamiliar to the modern reader.

It is for this reason that I have embarked upon this little book. It is not a translation of *The Cloud*. Neither is it a paraphrase or a commentary. It is an attempt to share the message of love found in *The Cloud* in a way easily understood by the men and women of today. It is an utterly simple book, as is *The Cloud of Unknowing*, inviting people into the beginnings of contemplative prayer. It is a message based on *The Cloud*, thoroughly imbued with *The Cloud's* teaching, and inspired by *The Cloud*.

I did not feel bound to repeat all that *The Cloud* contains or to limit myself only to what it contains. Chapters are omitted when I feel they are irrelevant and chapters are added when I feel they are helpful. I have avoided using direct quotations from *The Cloud* to avoid ending up by simply repeating the entire book, or most of it. Like *The Cloud*, this little book is divided into brief chapters, each with a descriptive title. With each title I have given a reference to *The Cloud* indicating what chapters from it are treated therein.

• *Byzantine Prayer*

Serene Light, shining in the
Ground of my being,
Draw me to yourself,
Draw me past the snares of the senses,
Out of the mazes of the mind,
Free me from symbols, from words,
That I may discover
  The Signified
  The Word Unspoken
In the darkness
That veils the ground of my being. Amen

· *Preface*

Child of God, this book is for you if you want it to be. If you love God or if you simply *want* to love God, this book is for you. Someone recently told me that, in her experience, religion was too often a matter of culture and not a matter of commitment. This explains, she said, why unloving things are done by churches, Christian communities, nations, and individuals. They have the veneer of Christianity but not the love that makes it real. If you feel in your heart that your commitment to God urges you to love, to discover what love is, to experience love, to share love and to receive love, please read this book and share it with others who feel the same.

[handwritten margin note: Show up as Love]

I gave a retreat once to a community of Poor Clare contemplative nuns. Toward the end of the retreat an elderly nun came in to see me. Bent over and crippled with age, she slowly walked across the room and painfully sat in the chair facing me. She sat for a while in silence. Suddenly I had a very powerful premonition that she was going to say something of great significance. She did! Nodding her head affirmingly, she looked at me and said, "Father, everything leads to God, everything, everything, everything!" We both sat there in silence, letting the full meaning of this wisdom sink in. I have still not exhausted its depth.

It means, dear friend in God, that we were made for love and that everything else was made to make love possible. If you agree with this and even if you have not been as actively engaged in the search for love as you might have wished, you can begin right now. Read this book, be encouraged and reassured in your loving pursuit, and invite others to do the same.

This book is divided into brief chapters to make reading easier and hopefully to allow intervals for reflection. It is about love, God's love for us, our love for God and for each other. You already know something of this love. Please continue to read and know more. Taste and see that the Lord is sweet.

• On the Three Levels of the Christian Life

(See chapter 1 of *The Cloud*)

Dear friend in God, there is a very old Christian tradition that recognizes three levels in the growth of a child of God as he or she matures in the loving search. They are sometimes called the three ways and they are: the purgative way, the illuminative way, and the unitive way.

From my observations I would say that people actually spend most of their lives between these ways. By that I mean that they sometimes are in two or even three of these stages or ways at the same time. They are, all three, stages in the process of loving God.

As in any journey, we must start at the beginning. This is the purgative way. We are aware of our attraction for God but perhaps, because of worldly attractions, habits of sin, moral weaknesses, or simple ignorance, we find ourselves now hot, now cold, in our loving search. We are just learning how to pray and our relationship to God is often expressed by memorized prayers or requests for help. Still it is a beginning. We must crawl before we can walk.

The second stage, the illuminative way, is really where contemplative prayer begins. Here we realize that God loves us and we fervently seek to love God in return. Religion is for us more than a culture: it becomes a genuine way of life. We can slip up once in a while and fall back into the purgative way, but we are willing to start over as often as it is necessary. We must walk before we can run.

The third stage is the unitive way. This is the way of the saints but nonetheless one to which we are all called. Often we have a foot (or even two) on this way, but do not realize it. Perhaps, dear friend, you may be reluctant to place yourself in such a high stage. You may tell yourself that you are not worthy, or that this third way is reserved only for special friends of God.

This is true. You *are not* worthy. This third way *is* reserved only for special friends of God. But do you not know that God calls you not because you are worthy but because God loves you? And because God loves you, you *are* a special friend of God. It is not pride to admit this: it is simple honesty. God is calling you to great holiness. It is not something that you have to earn. Jesus already did that for you. Just accept it and run towards the Lord with open arms and an eager heart. The kind of prayer characteristic of this third way is contemplative prayer. This little book will try to gently lead you on over the threshold of this loving union with God.

CHAPTER 2

• *A Word of Encouragement*

(See chapter 2 of *The Cloud*)

Dear friend, do not try to compare yourself with others, either saints or sinners. Do not say, "At least I am better than such and such a one," or "I could never be as holy as that one." Just be yourself. Stand before God in your need and with the love that God gives to you and be content. I do not mean be content in the sense of not wanting to love God more. I encourage you to continually seek to love God more. So in this way, you should never be content. But I do mean to be content to be who you are, a special friend of God called to holiness. You are not someone else, either saint or sinner, so forget making comparisons. Concentrate then on this wonderful love God has for you. It is freely given, not because you deserve it but because God wants to give it to you.

You have an exciting journey before you. I would like to go with you, to encourage you, and to remind you that the Lord can supply everything you need and protect you from every evil. Press on.

CHAPTER 3

• *The Beginning of Your Instructions on Contemplative Prayer*
(See chapter 3 of *The Cloud*)

Do you realize, dear friend in God, what a joy it is to love God? Do you realize what joy it gives to others when you love God? By others I mean not only God or the saints and angels, but all your brothers and sisters throughout the world who profit by your love. I will have a great deal more to say about this later.

When I took my solemn vows as a Trappist monk I meditated long and hard over my reasons for making such a commitment. After ten days of this in our little community hermitage out in the woods, I decided that I was becoming a monk because I loved God and was so caught up in the pursuit of that love that I had no time for other things—even other good things.

"Well," you may say, "but I am not called to be a monk or a nun." This may be true, dear friend in God, but you are called to be caught up in the same loving search—you may very well have to be a man or woman of action, involved in the great corporal and spiritual works of mercy, but even these have to be motivated by love. Do you know that what you do (your activity) springs from what you are (your being)? As the philosophers put it, action springs from being.

St. Augustine said, "Do whatever you want, as long as you love." He meant that if you are a loving human being, wholly given to the loving search for God, for others, and for yourself, there need be no concern that you will fall into sinful activity. So let love be your first concern, indeed your only concern, and everything else will fall into place.

This is how you should pray. Simply love God. Be in God's presence in that love. Do you remember the story of St. John Vianney and the old man? St. John was a village pastor in France. He was renowned as a holy and wise counselor and hundreds of people used to come to his church for confession. Each afternoon as he entered the church, he would see an elderly man sitting in a pew before the tabernacle. When he left the church several hours later, the man would still be there. One day, St. John went up to the man and asked, "What do you do sitting here all afternoon, day after day?" "I don't do anything," he replied. "I just look at God and God looks at me."

Please try to understand, dear friend of God, that when you love God you enter into the very heart of God. With this as your source, you then reach out and love all that God loves. When you first begin this loving search (which is, at the same time, a search and a discovery) you may be puzzled and even wonder if you are really praying. But leave it up to God. God calls you to love and you will soon experience that it is indeed God's grace that calls you. Later on I will give you some suggestions to facilitate this kind of simple, contemplative prayer.

CHAPTER 4

• *How Loving God Is Simply an Act of the Will*

(See chapter 4 of *The Cloud*)

Is it difficult to love God? How long does it take? Perhaps you have been discouraged by some lives of the saints or by spiritual accounts describing the journey toward God, which we are calling the loving search. This discouragement comes from the world, the flesh, and the devil. Do not give in to it. After all, what does it take to love God?

Actually, as far as you are concerned, you do not have what it takes to love God. It is a free gift that God gives you. So while you do not have it of yourself, just as you did not bring about your existence by yourself, you do have this grace, this gift. God constantly offers it to you. How long do you think it takes to love God? It takes but a moment. You have only to reach out and *will* to love God. You can do this whenever you wish (i.e., whenever you *will*) by simply lifting your heart *(will)* to God to embrace God in love. You can do this in silence or you can very simply say:

"God, I love you." It takes only a brief moment. When you do this, you will experience that it is not only very easy but that you will tend to want to repeat it again and again. Sometimes it will be just a brief act of love offered in the midst of a busy day spent in pursuit of the myriad activities of your life-calling. At other times you will want to sit quietly in God's presence repeating this act of love or simply savoring it.

Gradually you will find your day becoming more and more filled with this love, spilling over into all you do. When this happens, you are in what I would call the contemplative attitude. But you must remember that the contemplative attitude springs from the contemplative act—that is, lifting your will to God in response to God's grace in love. This takes but a moment. Do it now!

CHAPTER 5

• *How the Human Mind Is Like a Little House*

(See chapters 4, 5, and 6 of *The Cloud*)

Dear friend in God, there are many ways to understand the workings of the human mind. Philosophers have spent centuries trying to explain it. They have come up with lots of theories, which we call epistemologies. It is quite impossible to prove the objective truth of any one of them. They are merely descriptive of how the mind seems to work. Different epistemologies are useful depending upon what particular aspect of the human mind one is concerned with. For mental health, perhaps, one explanation is useful; for the educational process, perhaps another is to be preferred. For contemplation and for the loving search, which is our concern in this little book, we will use the epistemology of St. Augustine, St. Thomas Aquinas, St. Teresa of Avila, and St. John of the Cross. It is sometimes called the Scholastic epistemology.

This is my own way of explaining the Scholastic epistemology. You or others may have better ways. If so, please disregard what I say and remain with your own understanding of the matter.

The human mind has two major sources of activity: the intellect and the will. If you wish, you may see your mind as a little house with two connecting rooms. In each of these rooms dwells a little lady. One room is very bright with large, clear, sparkling windows open to the world outside. There is also a large door, usually open, to invite passers-by to have tea with the little lady who lives there and whom we will call Miss Intellect.

This little lady has very keen eyesight and is very quizzical. She is constantly on the watch for interesting travelers who might pass by her house so she can invite them in for tea and ask them questions.

CHAPTER 6

· Which Continues the Description of the Intellect Seeking Truth

(See chapter 5 of *The Cloud*)

Do you see, dear friend in God, that your intellect is interested in what is true? It is oriented toward the truth and, indeed, can only concern itself with what it thinks to be true. And so this little lady is constantly on the lookout for whatever her keen eyes tell her is true. Sometimes, of course, she may be deceived. This is why she invites truths to come in for tea—so she can question them and discover whether they are authentic or not. When she finds a real truth, she must accept it. She is not free to reject it but must invite it in for tea (and for questioning).

Let me show you a little experiment to prove that your intellect is directed toward the truth and is not free to reject it. "Two and two is four." Can you deny this? Are you free to reject this obvious truth and say, with sincerity, "No, two and two is eighteen?" Your intellect compels you to accept this truth even if you should wish to pretend otherwise. This is why people are often willing to die for the truth. Their personal integrity will not allow them to deny what their intellect perceives as true.

And so your Miss Intellect sits in her little tearoom, busy with all the truths that go by her windows, serving them tea (i.e., questioning them). If Miss Intellect is responsive to grace, she is especially interested in truths about God. She loves to invite the saints (through their biographies and their writings), the divine mysteries (through the sacraments and church doctrine and tradition), the word of God (through the Bible), and even the God-Made Manifest (through the humanity of Jesus). She is pleased to chat, to question, and to learn further truths from all of them. One great thing she does learn from them (even from the humanity of Jesus), is that their purpose is not to have her stop with them as though they were ultimate truths. Rather they all tell her that she must, with their help, go beyond all of them if she would bring her little house and all it involves (namely, you) to the ultimate truth.

Oh, how she longs for this ultimate truth, how she desires to have God visit her, not through messengers, but in the magnificence and simplicity of God's own being without intermediaries. She would so eagerly invite God in for a special tea. Her mind reels from imagining the truths God would reveal to her.

And then one day God comes and stands in her doorway! Miss Intellect does not invite God in. She cannot. In fact she cannot even see God. She is suddenly blinded. Not because it is dark, but because there is too much light. You see, dear friend of God, Miss Intellect is finite and limited. She can and does handle truths about God, but when God, the infinite truth, stands before her, she stops functioning, she cannot see, she simply lays down on her couch, and goes to sleep.

CHAPTER 7
· *Which Tells about the Will
and Its Search for the Good*
(See chapter 6 of *The Cloud*)

Ah, but the little house, which is your mind, remember, does not turn this infinite truth away. There is another room. Someone in that room has been waiting for the great moment. You see, Miss Intellect has a sister. Unfortunately, she is blind. Her room is connected to the brightly lit room of the intellect, but it is without lights and windows. She waits in her dark room for her sister, Miss Intellect, to open the door whenever she sees a truth and introduce that truth to her. Then Miss Will, for that is the blind sister, reaches out and embraces that truth in love. The will does not question a truth. She does not serve tea! She accepts the truth as the intellect presents it and loves it. The intellect seeks knowledge; the will seeks union.

When the intellect recognizes a truth, she presents it to the will. Miss Will is oriented to whatever is good in the same way that Miss Intellect is oriented to whatever is true. But whatever is true is also, by that very fact, good. So Miss Will, who is our loving power, allows Miss Intellect to be her eyes because love is blind.

The problem the intellect has—the inability to receive infinite truth—is not a problem for the will. She is quite capable, with the help of grace, to reach out and embrace infinite good. She, indeed, is the power by which we are able to receive union with God.

To reach the point we are now at, and which is the basic experience of contemplative prayer, we must first do some searching. Indeed the intellect has been doing this for us, learning all she could about God. But she also realized this important fact: truths about God are not themselves God. They lead to God, but are in fact, as theologians tell us, infinitely removed from God. If we would seek union with God, we must go beyond the truths about God to the truth itself. The truths of the intellect show us the way. The embrace of the will, under grace, brings about the union.

CHAPTER 8

· Which Talks about the Negative Approach

(See chapter 7 of *The Cloud*)

Perhaps now, dear friend in God, you can understand the approach to God taught in this little book, and which I sometimes call the negative approach. Perhaps the most well-known theologian of this negative approach is St. John of the Cross. He constantly re-

minds his readers of the catchword of the negative approach—
Nothing . . . Nothing . . . Nothing. That is, nothing but God.

There is, of course, a paradox here, because when you have union
with God, you have union with everything God has made and
loves. That is why the prayer that seeks this union, contemplative
prayer, cannot be concerned with anything less than God. It is not
in itself a prayer for favors, an expression of sorrow, or a petition
for suffering souls. It does not involve considerations on church
teaching, the Bible, the lives of the saints, or even the sacraments.
It does rely on all of these to be brought to fruition and uses
them in their own very important times and places. But in the
contemplative dimension, seeking union with God, it goes beyond
all of them and seeks Nothing . . . Nothing . . . Nothing . . . but
God. To be satisfied with anything else is to be satisfied with less
than God.

I speak here, dear friend, of a great mystery. It may be beyond
your understanding but not beyond your embrace. You have God's
grace, God's power, God's invitation to the loving search. Indeed,
we are told that we could not search for God unless we had already
found God. We are brought to God by realizing what God has
done for us. We remain with God in contemplative love because of
what God is in Godself.

Let me conclude this chapter with a word about the value of this
kind of prayer to the church and, indeed, to the whole world. It
is much more valuable and efficacious than any explicit, external
prayers begging for God's kindness to manifest itself on our needs
or those of others.

CHAPTER 9

• *How the Loving Will Can Be
Distracted by the Memory, the
Imagination, and the Intellect*
(See chapters 7 and 8 of *The Cloud*)

It will often happen when you seek to embrace God alone in the
dark chamber of your loving power, the will, that her sister the
intellect will actually interfere. She does not at all understand what
is going on. She cannot see the infinite good that the will embraces
and tries to continue helping the will in her customary way—by
offering her limited truths, which are, as we have said, less than
God. These are truths that the will is not interested in right then
because she is in union with the infinite good.

And there are two more sisters in this little house, which is your
mind, whom we have not yet introduced. They live in two little
rooms in the basement and are called Miss Memory and Miss Imagination. They are quite friendly with Miss Intellect and often help
her serve tea to guests (and question them). Miss Memory spends
much time in her little room downstairs, going over old photo
albums of former visitors to the tearoom. Every so often, sometimes very often, she runs upstairs with her photos to show them
around—especially at those times when her sister the intellect is
somewhat quiet.

The fourth sister, Miss Imagination, sits in her basement room
with reels and reels of filmstrips. She is constantly cutting and
splicing old films to make new and interesting pictures. She is also
constantly running upstairs to show her latest creations.

It is to be expected then that when your will is seeking to embrace
God in love and your intellect is somewhat quiet, these two sisters,
Miss Memory and Miss Imagination, will try to do their thing. Let
me give you some advice on how to deal with all three of them in
order to leave the will free to love. The clamorous activity of these
sisters during contemplative meditation is often spoken of as "interior noise." This kind of noise can be a much greater distraction

than exterior noises. We speak, of course, of the frequent problem of interior distractions. Let me give you some advice on how to deal with all three of these bothersome sisters in order to leave the will free to love.

CHAPTER 10

· Which Contains a Suggestion Regarding a Prayer Word and How to Deal with Distraction

(See chapters 7 and 8 of *The Cloud*)

When you wish to spend some time in contemplative prayer, dear friend in God, please realize that this very wish itself is a grace and an invitation from God. Many people find it helpful to choose a prayer word to aid them in this loving search and process.

What do I mean by a prayer word? I mean, choose a name of God that you feel comfortable with and invest that name with all the love you have for God. Then in your heart (not with your voice), peacefully, allow that prayer word to repeat itself and listen to it with the ear of your soul.

In my experience, many people choose the prayer word "Abba, Father." Others like other names of God such as Lord, Jesus, Savior, Holy Spirit, Yahweh, Kyrios, Adonai.

Let this name be the symbol and expression of your love for God. Sit quietly and listen to this prayer word repeat itself in your heart. As you do this, your will is reaching out (or within if you wish) to embrace God in love. Whenever your intellect or memory or imagination enters and tries to distract you, just gently focus on this prayer word and use it to chase away the distractions it tries to present. Contemplative loving of God is that simple. Try it.

Dear friend in God, let me say just a word about those who object to the use of a prayer word. Their arguments usually proceed from a fear that this prayer word is actually a mantra, a kind of word-sound used by Hindu and Buddhist monks in their meditation. I really do not know much about mantras, so I cannot com-

ment on them. I do know that the use of a prayer word is found
in the most ancient teachings of our holy church. It is taught by
wise men and women, saints and mystics, with the approval of the
church and I strongly recommend it. Let those who are afraid of
mantras deal with mantras. I am not concerned about it, and have
nothing further to say to them.

CHAPTER 11
· *A Consideration of the Place of the
Intellect, the Memory, and the
Imagination in Our Prayer Life*
(See chapters 8 and 9 of *The Cloud*)

Now, dear friend in God, you may ask me: "What is wrong
with my intellect presenting me with ideas about God? What is
wrong with my memory recalling past acts of God's love and
mercy? What is wrong with my imagination presenting me with
images of the crucifixion or the risen Christ or the saints and
angels?"

I will answer you. There is nothing wrong with it at all. However, please try to understand that there are levels or degrees in
your prayer life that must be considered. In the beginning levels—
the purgative way and in part of the illuminative way—you need
your intellect to know about God. You need your intellect to meditate on the Bible, church teachings, and traditions, and on their
applications to your life. Memory and imagination also are important here.

But, dear friend, there comes a time when you will be called
from knowing *about* God to actually knowing God—that is, embracing God in love. You will be told, "Taste and see that the Lord
is sweet," or "Peace, be still, and know that I am God." It is at
these times that your imagination, your memory, and your intellect
must be abandoned, and your will be allowed to love even if in
darkness.

When children are infants, they drink only milk. Then, as they grow, they go on to soft foods and finally meat or whatever a grown person eats. But even the grown person will continue to have milk or milk products. But then it will have a different place in their eating habits as their need for milk changes. At no time will they completely abandon it. So it is with earlier forms of prayer, using memory, imagination, and intellect. You will be called to go beyond them. They will play a different part in your life as you grow spiritually. You will always need them, always have a use for them, but you will also have richer food, indeed, the very source of life itself, in the loving search that is contemplative prayer.

So, dear friend, you do not have to be concerned and think that I am advising you to stop reading the Bible or spiritual books— indeed, am I not here presenting you with yet another book to read? You must not think that I am telling you to stop saying the rosary, or the psalms, or singing hymns of praise or thanksgiving. Of course I am not saying that. I am saying, however, that these kinds of prayer, at times, will give way to the simple loving of God, which is true contemplation. Indeed, you will often find that these kinds of prayers will actually lead you into this simple loving of God. When this happens, do not resist it. Allow yourself to cease saying the rosary, or praying the psalms, or meditating on the Bible, and to enter into the peaceful loving of God beyond words, thoughts, and imaginings.

Do not think that you are wasting your time because you are not involved in mental calculations. Do not think that you are being idle because you are resting in loving contemplation of God. It is at these times that you are being most faithful to what you are and what you are called to be: a lover in union with the beloved.

CHAPTER 12

• On the Kinds of Thoughts That Can
Arise to Disturb Your Simple, Loving
Search for God

(See chapters 9 and 10 of The Cloud)

Please recall, dear friend in God, my example of your mind being
a little house with four sisters in four rooms—memory, imagination, intellect, and will. One of the functions of Miss Intellect is,
on occasion, to lock the basement doors of Miss Memory and
Miss Imagination simply because they have so many photos and
filmstrips they want to show. They would forever be clattering
about and showing this or recalling that, and never giving you a
moment's peace. Also, at times, they can be quite insensitive and
bring up memories or pictures that Miss Intellect would rather keep
locked up. So it is that Miss Intellect, sometimes with the firm aid
of Miss Will, censors what she allows them to bring up and reveal.
She also limits it in terms of quantity, lest it become quite
overwhelming.

It often happens that when Miss Will in her little dark room is
engaged in the loving search for God and Miss Intellect is sleeping
on her couch (as there is, at the moment, nothing for her to do),
Miss Memory and Miss Imagination will sneak past her and enter
Miss Will's room. They will then seek to distract her from her
reaching out to God in love. Usually they will bring up whatever
interests them at the moment and whatever is current.

CHAPTER 13

⋆ *Which Concerns Even Sinful Thoughts*
(See chapter 13 of *The Cloud*)

Sometimes Miss Memory has lists of things you should be doing or have forgotten to do. Sometimes Miss Imagination will draw you pictures of wonderful projects you could accomplish or even sinfully attractive things that might beguile you. St. Teresa of Avila tells her novices that when this happens, they should simply laugh it off. What she means is, do not take it too seriously. What I would tell you is, just ignore them and go on with your loving prayer word or go back to it if you find that you have stopped it to listen to your uninvited visitors. Do this as often as necessary, even many times in a short period. It does not matter. Each time you go back to your loving prayer word, you are reaffirming your love for God.

It may happen, dear friend in God, that sometimes memory or imagination may bring up something that is important and must absolutely be dealt with by summoning Miss Intellect and taking up a discussion with her. When this seems to be necessary, just go ahead and do it. You can continue your loving prayer word another time. This will not happen with great frequency.

CHAPTER 14

⋆ *How the Loving Search Touches and Changes Our Inmost Being.*
The "Method" of Contemplative Prayer
(See chapter 12 of *The Cloud*)

Dear friend, now that you have begun your loving search, do not give up. Do keep in mind that love begins when nothing is expected in return. In this prayer of love we seek nothing—that is, nothing less than God who is everything. Remember also that God will not be outdone in generosity. God will work in you wonderful things as a result of your loving search.

Jesus said that it is not what goes into persons that should concern them but what comes out of them. I think, if you are anything like me, you know well that the good that you want to do, you often do not do, and the evil that you do not want to do, is what you end up doing (as St. Paul reminds us). It seems sometimes that no matter how hard you try, you find yourself falling into the same old patterns of sins. Please try to realize that any sin, whether serious or "light," is actually an act of unloving. It is the opposite of loving. When we sin it is a sin precisely because it involves an unloving act, toward God, toward neighbor, or toward ourselves.

What a consolation it is to know that our loving search for God in contemplative prayer is just the opposite of unloving and it strengthens us, starting from the very core of our being, to become loving persons. I once heard a Hindu wise man say, "To get the fruit, water the root." What he meant was that if we want to be truly loving persons, we must permit the love to come forth from the very heart of our being. Only then will we find that our actions, which proceed from our loving being, will consistently be loving actions. Sometimes this is the only way we can get rid of annoying and hitherto unshakable habits of unloving acts.

Loving union with God destroys sin and the causes of sin at their very roots. It is probably more effective in rooting out sin than thousands of resolutions and personal attempts to avoid habitual, unloving deeds. God is the source of love, the *only* source of love. When we seek union with the source of love, we ourselves become intermediaries of that love as it proceeds through us from the divine source out into our individual worlds.

Dear friend in God, permit me at this point to spell out for you concretely the method I would offer you for your contemplative meditation.

1) Sit comfortably in a quiet place where you are not liable to be interrupted. Place your feet flat on the floor and keep your hands loosely folded in your lap or flat on your knees. It is better to use a chair with a moderately soft covering and without close fitting arms. Your eyes should be closed and your head held at a

comfortable angle. If you have some illness or physical disability, sit or lie in whatever way that suits your condition.

2) Take a moment to relax. It is helpful to take three deep breathes. Fill your lungs by expanding your stomach. Hold the breath for about five seconds and then slowly exhale. Do this three times. I usually do this with a very brief prayer to each person of the Blessed Trinity. First breath: "In the name of the Father;" second: "In the name of the Son;" third: "In the name of the Holy Spirit."

3) Say a brief prayer in your own words expressing your love for God and your desire to spend these few moments embracing God in your love. Let it be something like this:

> Dear Father in heaven, I love you. I want to love you more. I know that you love me and you have given me the grace to want to spend these twenty minutes in your presence. I have chosen the prayer word (Abba, Father, or whatever word you have chosen) to express this love I have for you. In the power of your Holy Spirit and united to your son, Jesus Christ, I will now offer you my love through this prayer.

4) Next, calmly, peacefully, and lovingly listen with the ears of your heart to your prayer word as you allow it silently to repeat itself. Do not whisper it out loud or even use your tongue or lips. Realize that by this word you are expressing your love for God. Continue to do this fifteen or twenty minutes or longer if you feel called to do so.

5) Whenever distractions come (Miss Imagination or Miss Memory) and you find that you have given in to them and allowed your prayer word to stop, simply say: "I will go back to my prayer word," and do so. Do this as often as is necessary—even many, many times during a twenty-minute meditation.

6) If, during this prayer of your loving search, you should fall asleep, just thank God for the blessing of sleep and go back to your prayer word. Do not be concerned about this—God is not!

7) Sometimes you will "transcend" your prayer word. That is, your will will be silently loving God in her dark chamber, your prayer word will have stopped, and you will be in silent repose,

loving God without words and without symbols. This is fine. When you realize that you have done this, just say: "I will go back to my prayer" and do so. Time will pass very quickly when this happens.

8) When you think your time is up, look at your watch. If you still have a few minutes, go back to your prayer until twenty minutes is up. Then very slowly begin to say the Our Father, so that it takes you a full two minutes to say it. If you find that you would like to go back to your loving prayer, and you have the time, do so; otherwise your prayer is finished.

I hope you will realize, dear friend in God, that this chapter is very important. In many ways, most of the rest of this book depends upon it, and will serve to explain and facilitate it.

Go boldly forward into this prayer. Make it your own. Then continue to read this book for further understanding and assistance.

CHAPTER 15

• *Some Ideas about a Very Unpopular Virtue—Humility*

(See chapter 13 of *The Cloud*)

Dear friend of God, we are often told by spiritual masters that humility is the foundation of the spiritual life. If we truly desire to love God and to engage in the loving search that is contemplation, we must seek from God growth in humility.

In our world today (and perhaps it has always been so) humility is the least popular of the virtues. Yet without it, we can never get off the ground in our loving search. True humility is so difficult that it can be practiced only when it comes from God. But please try to remember that with God nothing is impossible. God's yoke is sweet, God's burden light.

It is not surprising that humility is so little understood. I was once told by a so-called theologian that humility consisted in knowing where you were but in acting as if you were a degree or two lower. This is absurd. According to this idea, humility consists basically in a deceit, in pretending you are less than you know yourself to be!

No, dear friend, you are humble when you know yourself as you truly are and when you are willing to look this truth in the face and accept it. Here is where your little lady in the tearoom comes in again. Recall that she is constantly seeking the truth. She is always on the lookout for the truth. When she finds one passing by her open door, she invites it in for tea (i.e., questioning). You can see, can you not, that one very important truth she must invite in and question is the truth about yourself.

Here are some questions she must ask. What kind of a person are you? What do other people think of you? How much truth is in what they say? What things get you angry, embarrassed, sad, humiliated? How adequate are you to face the tasks of your present state of life? How do you treat those around you on a daily basis? How do you deal with those who love you? Can you accept help or criticism? Do you have a low self-esteem or an overhigh one? What things do you avoid that you should be facing? And many, many other such questions.

If you are not used to this kind of self-examination, you may be prone to answer these questions in a very self-satisfied way and conclude that you are not really so bad after all. Or you may go to the other extreme, and judge yourself as a total failure. Neither of these conclusions is the fruit of humility.

CHAPTER 16

• *Humility Is the Truth about Yourself*
(See chapter 13 of *The Cloud*)

If you have the true humility that comes from God, you will know the truth about yourself and that truth will set you free. You will know that as a creature, as a human being, you belong to a fallen race. You are one of a large community of intelligent beings called to be sons and daughters of God, but whose fallen nature tends toward deceit, self-interest, lust, and power. As you are in yourself and without God's grace, you are less than nothing. When you allow your intellect free reign to examine the truth about yourself, you will see how you manifest these negative and sinful attitudes in your daily life.

However, do not be discouraged, because the truth does not end there. No, besides being a member of a fallen race, you are a member of a redeemed, holy people. You belong to the body of Christ and have been brought back to the Father by the death and resurrection of his Son and the working of the Holy Spirit. You have the promise of a glorious future, both in this world and the next. God has bent over and lifted you from the mire of a fallen people and clasped you to God's own bosom in a nourishing, protecting embrace of love.

To know the truth, we have to recognize both sides of ourselves. We must try to realize how we show in our lives the weaknesses of our fallen nature and, at the same time, glory in our redemption by Jesus and our return to the Father by the Holy Spirit.

We must try to recognize our constant efforts to glorify ourselves apart from God. We have to examine that false self that we create contrary to God's image and likeness. We must see the daily power struggles we engage in to influence other people unfairly. We must know that we make use of anger, lies, despair, sorrow, threats, jealousy, fear, bribery, and a thousand other wicked devices to gain control over our lives and the lives of others.

But remember, dear friend in God, the other side of the coin. When we are engaged in the loving search for God, we are also engaged in the loving search for our true selves. By embracing God in a union of love in the prayer of contemplation, we are gradually led by God to know our true selves. We come to know what we are like with all of our weaknesses and what we would be like without God's grace. We come also to know who we are as God's beloved sons and daughters. This is true humility. Go for it!

CHAPTER 17

* *In Which We Consider Further the Relationship between True Humility and the Loving Search*

(See chapters 15 and 16 of *The Cloud*)

There are, dear friend, two ways to practice humility. One way is to attempt to control our actions (including the action of thinking) so that they are in accord with our understanding of the virtue of humility. This is often, and laudably, done by recalling our past, its sins, imperfections, and failures. This is all right as far as it goes, but there are some cautions to be observed.

In the first place, there are some people (perhaps you are one of them; I know that I am not) who do not have a past that is filled with sins, imperfections, and failures. How can they be humble? Jesus said, "Learn of me for I am meek and humble of heart." Certainly Jesus had no sins, yet he was humble. So we can see that even good and holy people must be humble. We shall see how in a moment.

In the second place, there are some people who have a low self-esteem and who are even willing to wallow in the mire of their sinful past. These people tend to exaggerate their failures and weaknesses, and say, "It is no wonder I am a miserable, wretched person. I have such a miserable past. What can you expect from such a degraded, debased human being as I? Woe is me!" Such people love the false trappings of humility because they allow self-pity and also support their low self-esteem.

Both of these types, I tell you, have got to find their humility in the loving search. Yes, both must be sorry for past sins. Yes, both must be aware of their sinful nature. But also both must acknowledge divine forgiveness and their own elevation to the status of children of God. Both are called to the contemplative embrace of a loving God where they will experience forgiveness and union. In this way and from this source, they will be led to know who they are in truth. They will be led to humility through love. Jesus will teach them.

CHAPTER 18

· Which Tells about Jesus and His Friends in Bethany

(See chapter 17 of *The Cloud*)

Dear friend in God, I am writing this little book from the Trappist monastery of Latroun in the Holy Land. This monastery is located between Tel Aviv and Jerusalem. As I look out my front window, I can see over the broad plain of the Ayalon Valley, where Joshua once held back the sun by his prayer.

Over in the distance I see the town of Lydda. This was, in the third century, the home of St. George and the place of his martyrdom. In the first century, it was the town where St. Peter went after Pentecost and where he healed the cripple, Aeneas, as told in the Acts of the Apostles. I can also look toward the hill country going up to Jerusalem. The monastery itself is located in a very holy place. It was built on the site of the ancient city of Emmaus. This is where the two disciples, on Easter Sunday, listened to Jesus explain the scriptures and where they recognized him in the breaking of the bread.

Because of the location of the monastery, I have easy access to many of the holy places where our Lord visited and carried out his redemptive mysteries. One of these places, only an hour away, which I visited a few days ago, is the town of Bethany. It is barely a half-hour's walk from Jerusalem, and it was here that Jesus usually stayed with his friends, Lazarus, Martha, and Mary, when he came up to Jerusalem for the important feast days.

Just off the main road, which continues down to Jericho and the Dead Sea only seven miles to the west, I visited the beautiful little church which marks the site of the home of Jesus' friends. I was privileged to be able to offer Mass there and to read the gospel account on the very spot where Jesus once sat and taught his disciples with Mary sitting at his feet, rapt in loving wonderment. I could almost see and hear the busy Martha standing at the doorway, arms akimbo and insisting that Jesus send Mary into the kitchen to help her prepare dinner.

The words of Jesus echoed and reechoed through the Gothic arches of this little church as they have done in this place and throughout the world for twenty centuries. "Martha, Martha, you are worried and upset about many things, but only one thing is needed; Mary has chosen what is better and it will not be taken away from her."

CHAPTER 19
• *How We are Combinations of Martha and Mary*
(See chapter 17 of *The Cloud*)

The church has always seen this beautiful gospel story as symbolic of the contemplative and the active aspects of the loving search. Mary, of course, is the contemplative. She sits at the feet of Jesus and adores. Martha serves Jesus too, but in a different way. She is preparing dinner. She does not understand why Mary is allowed to remain with Jesus and sit at his feet when there are so many things to be done.

My friend, in our loving search, we are neither Martha nor Mary. We are both. There are times when we are called to be loving God in the union of contemplative prayer, and there are times when we have to be busy about many things serving our brethren. Yet we must admit that Jesus, while certainly recognizing the need for both of these aspects, gives a preference to the loving, to Mary. This, he tells Martha, is the better part.

There is, of course, a good reason for this and we have already spoken to you about it. The loving is primary and the activity must proceed from the loving. Remember, I told you that activity proceeds from being. Certainly there are times when Mary must work in the kitchen—but not when God calls her to some special time in the loving search, sitting at his feet in contemplative prayer. Martha, too, must do this, if her service is to be truly loving. The place of this loving prayer will be different in the lives of different people and it will even differ in the life of one person from time to time, depending upon where he or she is in the loving search.

CHAPTER 20

• *Which Takes Us on a Visit to Bethlehem*

(See chapter 20 of *The Cloud*)

Another holy place that I sometimes visit is the town of Bethlehem. There, up the hill about a fifteen-minute walk from the church of the Nativity, where Jesus was born, is a lovely Carmelite convent. Attached to the convent is a large hostelry for pilgrims and visitors to Bethlehem. Several times a year small groups of about twelve American Maryknoll missionary priests and brothers come there for a spiritual renewal program. These are men who have been working, sometimes for thirty or forty years, in mission countries all over the world. To each group that has come for the past year, I have given a kind of retreat-workshop in contemplative prayer, according to the manner described in *The Cloud of Unknowing* and repeated in this little book.

The director of the program, Father William Galvin, promotes these retreats among the members of his society. He calls them "Contemplative Prayer for Busy People." It is busy people, above all, who must take the time to sit at the feet of Jesus in the loving search if their business is to be a product of love.

Some years ago there was a very popular slogan, which ran: "Where there is no love, put love and you will find love." Love comes from contemplative union with God. Seek after love and pursue it. This little book describes at least one very important way to do this.

I am a Trappist monk. For thirty years I have belonged to the Cistercian (Trappist) Order, commonly and canonically acknowledged to be one of the "contemplative orders." Yet, dear friend, I would be the first to deny that my order consists exclusively of Marys! It is not possible to live in any Christian human context without engaging in loving service of one another. We monks realize, perhaps better than most, that we are all combinations of Martha and Mary. Yes, we spend much of our time sitting at the feet of Jesus as we sing the divine office, study the Scriptures and the church fathers, and enter into the darkness of the cloud in our contemplative meditations.

But we also spend a great deal of time in loving service of one another by cooking, laundry, infirmary work, farming, and housekeeping, as well as caring for guests and retreatants. Like the Maryknoll missionaries who seek to allow their work throughout the world, their being about their Father's business, to spring from their contemplative love in its various forms, so too, we Trappists have to allow our sitting at the feet of Jesus to express itself in service and activity. And so, each in his or her own way, do we all.

CHAPTER 21

· *How Martha and Mary Complement One Another*

(See chapter 21 of *The Cloud*)

We are all, dear friend, combinations of Martha and Mary. Sometimes we lean more toward the one than toward the other. Sometimes we opt for permanent lifestyles that emphasize one over the other, such as the Trappists and the Maryknollers. There is one thing we must understand, however, and that is that our love must dominate our action and give it direction. This means, of course, that we must support one another. We must never criticize one tendency as being inferior or less Christian than the other. Remember how St. Paul tells us that love is patient and kind. It does not envy or boast. It is not proud, rude, self-seeking, easily angered, nor does it keep records of wrongdoings. Love protects, trusts, hopes, and perseveres.

CHAPTER 22
• *Which Is Concerned with the Modern Heresy of Activism*
(See chapter 23 of *The Cloud*)

Dear friend in God, we come from a society that is frenetic in its activity. It is caught up in the trauma of future shock. All it thinks about is speed, production, wealth, and material gain. Do not be surprised if you should find yourself the victim of criticism, even from some good people, when you seek to give yourself to the quiet and the dark cloud of contemplative prayer. As Martha did not understand Mary, many people will not understand your loving search. They will even criticize your meditation practice of gently going into God's presence in love by a quiet listening to your prayer word as a symbol of your union with God. To such people you are not really praying if you are not externally active or, at the very least, caught up in a flurry of mental activity and intellectual speculation.

Pay them no mind, I tell you. Simply do what Mary did. Continue to sit quietly at the feet of Jesus in love. Give yourself regularly to your contemplative meditation for perhaps fifteen or twenty minutes each time—more, if you wish. You do not have to defend yourself. You can do what Mary did—just remain silent and let Jesus defend you.

Please remember that starting over again every day is a wonderful form of perseverance in the loving search. God will never abandon you. Do not abandon God.

CHAPTER 23

• How in Contemplative Prayer We Love God for God's Own Sake but in Loving God, We Love Everybody

(See chapters 24 and 25 of *The Cloud*)

Friend, it is really so very simple. God loves you; just love God in return. Do this and everything else will be added unto you. Give the priority of your life to whom it belongs, to God.

When we practice the simple meditation of contemplative prayer, we love God for Godself alone. We have no other motive. We seek no personal favors, no consolations. We do not pray for anything, not for the church, not for our friends, not for sinners. Simply, Nothing . . . Nothing . . . Nothing—but loving God.

When we do this, dear friend, something very interesting happens. When we seek to love God above all things with our whole mind, heart, and strength, as Jesus tells us, that love spills over and we soon discover that we are also in God, loving our neighbor and ourselves. This is why when Jesus was asked what was the one great commandment, he had to give two commandments. He said, "The second commandment is like the first: love your neighbor as yourself for the love of God."

Even though during the actual time of your meditation you give no thought to your brothers or sisters, friends or enemies, you are actually reaching out in God and loving them in God. Remember, Jesus said that it was *for the love of God* that you loved your neighbor and yourself.

Also, dear friend in God, can you see now why Jesus insists that we must love our enemies. Just as no one is specifically mentioned or adverted to in our loving search for God in our contemplative meditation, so also no one is excluded. We embrace and love everyone whom God loves. No one is left out. No one can remain our enemy.

CHAPTER 24

• *Which Encourages You to Contemplative Prayer in Spite of the Difficulties*

(See chapter 26 of *The Cloud*)

Dear friend, I am not deceiving you. I have said that loving God is very simple, even easy. You know this yourself. At the same time I must tell you that it can be difficult. Sometimes you find yourself, in response to God's grace, sinking quietly into the loving peacefulness of God's presence. You are at peace and still, knowing that God is God. You taste and see that the Lord is sweet. You wait for God as the watchman waits for the dawn. You long for God as the deer longs for the waters of a sparkling stream. And God comes—and you love God and bask in God's love, quietly, without words, often without even the symbolic word of your love, your prayer word. Just you and God; and sometimes not even you, just God.

Yet at other times it is not like that at all. You go apart to spend twenty minutes loving God by gently listening to your prayer word, and your mind seems to be a turmoil of activity. The little sisters dwelling in your mind will not settle down. Miss Imagination and Miss Memory are running back and forth with their photo albums and filmstrips. Even Miss Intellect wakes up and attempts to carry on business as usual. Your poor will, seeking to love God, whom she knows to be present in her dark chamber, is beset with a barrage of distractions that never seem to end.

A few chapters further on, I am going to give you some concrete advice on how to deal with these problematic ladies, but, first, I have something else to tell you.

CHAPTER 25

• *The Loving Search Is More a Work of God than of You. Some More Comments on its Difficulty*

(See chapter 26 of *The Cloud*)

I remember many years ago, as a young novice, I went to the abbot in a very complaining mood. "Look," I said, "God loves me and I love God. Why should it be so difficult? Why can't we just get together?" At the time, I was having a great deal of difficulty in my loving search. The abbot smiled sadly. How many times had he been asked this same question?

I wanted a simple answer, two or three sentences that would solve everything. It would make life so much easier! Since that time I too have been asked frequently that question. The answer, as I now understand it, requires an explanation of the entire spiritual journey, the whole of the loving search from beginning to end.

I did not, however, leave the abbot empty-handed. Rather, I was much encouraged by what he said. Let me share it with you, dear friend in God. I will try to keep it as simple and brief as possible.

You see, if you desire to love God, to meet and embrace God in the loving union of contemplative prayer, it means that God desires this union also. The invitation came from God; it was not your idea at all. It has always been the teaching of the church that we cannot begin a movement toward God unless God begins that movement. We are told by God in the book of Isaiah, "Before you call upon me, I say to you, here I am."

Is that not wonderful? Before we call upon God in prayer, God is already present to us, empowering us by the grace of the Holy Spirit to seek God. This is what I mean when I say that the loving search is, first of all, God's search for us. When we respond to it, it then becomes our search for God. This is also what I mean when I say, "You could not search for God unless you had already found God."

When you understand this, what difference does it make how

much you have to struggle? You know it is worth it. You know who calls you, who accompanies you, and who is at the end of your loving search. Listen to God say to you in your difficulties, "Come to me all you who labor and are heavy burdened and I will give you rest. My yoke is sweet and my burden light." This is what the saints mean when they tell us, "The road to heaven *is* heaven."

Be generous then with your efforts, your perseverance, your starting over again as often as is necessary. Know that you are tilling the soil and that your work is worthwhile, because God will come and plant the seed. He will also see to its growth and its yield of thirty and sixty and one hundred fold. God wants to give you no less than Godself. Should you give God less than yourself?

CHAPTER 26
· *Who Should Engage in the Loving Search?*
(See chapter 27 of *The Cloud*)

I come, dear friend, on my mother's side from an Irish background. From her I learned the Irish custom of answering a question by posing yet another question. Who should engage in this loving search? My answering question is, Whom does God love? For whom did Jesus die? Who are God's children? Who is called to a union of eternal love with God in heaven? Does that answer the question for you? Does it include yourself?

CHAPTER 27
• What Is Required to Take up the Loving Search?
(See chapter 28 of *The Cloud*)

I do not think that anyone would be interested in contemplative union with God unless he or she was attempting to be truly devout and faithful in the practice of their religion. As a Catholic priest and monk, I presume that my primary audience is made up of Catholics. But I hope and fervently pray that it does not stop there. Remember all of God's children are called to the loving search. I ardently desire to accompany anyone of them, of whatever religion or even with no religion at all, in his or her loving search. The church has told us that even atheists who sincerely search for the truth are searching for God (Second Vatican Council—Document on Atheism).

What is required to take up the loving search, to begin the contemplative prayer of loving union with God? The answer is, of course, a devout and sincere adherence to one's faith, manifesting itself in fidelity to the commandments, obedience to Christ and his church, and regular reception of the sacraments. It is not required that we be perfect, sinless, without fault. It is required that we be willing to begin over again as often as we see that we have fallen. A real Christian, as opposed to a cultural Christian, is not one who never sins. He or she is one who, having sinned, is willing to reach out and find his or her sufficiency in Christ and start over again—today!

CHAPTER 28

· *In the Loving Search We See Things from the Heart of God*

(See chapter 23 of *The Cloud*)

What a glorious thing it is, dear friend, to enter into the heart of God! From this source and center of love, we return to work out whatever is required for our salvation and whatever is asked of us toward the salvation of the world. When we operate from the heart of God, we proceed from and together with the Son of God, and God's work of salvation is carried out in the love of the Holy Spirit. We become Christic, we become Christ, we become truly Christians. In God's mercy and through God's love, we learn more and more to view the world through the eyes of the risen Christ. We learn to love everyone, even (and, perhaps, especially?) inveterate sinners. We do not see sinners as people to be despised or condemned, but as children of God, called to love and holiness. We deplore the deeds of sin; we hate the sin but we love the sinner. This is so, even (and, perhaps, especially?) when we have been their victims. Then are we truly conformed to Christ when we can say with him, "Father, forgive them for they know not what they do," and then die (or, what may be harder, live) for them.

CHAPTER 29

• On the Difficulty of Forgiving
(See chapter 30 of *The Cloud*)

Many apparently sincere Christians will tell you how hard it is to forgive. Maybe they can forgive evil done to themselves, but find it impossible to forgive evil done to others, especially to those they love. I know of an apparently sincere, Christian woman, very active in the church and in all its external observances, who has not spoken to her own sister in twenty years. They parted ways in a dispute over their mother's will and neither will forgive the other. I know of a father, to all intents a practicing Catholic, who has not communicated with his son for ten years because his son became a monk instead of taking over the family business.

I call these people "apparently sincere Christians" because they do perform all the externals of their religion. They go to Mass, receive communion, support the church, help the poor, educate the ignorant, bury the dead, and the like. But they are lacking in the one thing necessary. I do not condemn them. There, but for the grace of God, go I! I have not known their temptations, their disappointments, their despair.

CHAPTER 30

• How Forgiveness Is Possible through God's Love

And yet I know the solution. It may very well be humanly impossible for them to forgive. They are not able simply to make an act of the will and go on intellectually and emotionally as if they had never been wounded at all. No, this requires something greater than themselves. If only they could be brought to understand. They have someone greater than themselves. They can forgive, not from their own meager and limited love, but from the unlimited compassion of God's love. They must enter into the heart of God in the loving search of contemplative prayer. Only then can they go full circle and return to the world, imbued with the love of Christ and empowered with the grace of the Holy Spirit. Only then can they be brought to forgive, not of their own power, but from God's. This, dear friend, is what we mean when we say, "To forgive is divine!"

CHAPTER 31

• *Dealing with Distractions*

(See chapter 31 of *The Cloud*)

In the contemplative prayer of our loving search, dear friend, we are, as I have said, often troubled by our memory and imagination. Often these troubling thoughts have to do with unpleasant past events in our lives—things we have done or things done to us. They can be very minor things like embarrassing moments, or traumatic things like childhood abuse. As a general rule, the time we allow for contemplative prayer is not the time for these thoughts. There are always exceptions to this but exceptions should not become the rule. I hope to share with you later some ways of dealing positively with these memories.

For beginners like you and me, dear friend, here is something we can try. Look to God. After all, this is what we are concerned with in the loving search, is it not? Do not attack the distracting thoughts directly. When you do this, you honor them. You give them attention. You leave off your prayerful union with God and invite your intellect, memory, and imagination into the chamber of your heart. Even your will decides to change course and give consent to these distractions. God is forgotten while we wrestle with these uninvited visitors.

No, I beg of you, this is not the way to deal with them. Give them no notice at all. Look over their shoulders as though they were people standing in your way when you were trying to give your attention to something (or somebody) behind them. Do not honor them with your attention.

If they still continue to bother you, as they sometimes will, just quietly allow your love, as symbolized by your prayer word, to issue forth from your heart as peacefully and gently as you can. If you discover that you have, without realizing it, stopped your prayer word to engage these thoughts, simply say to yourself, "I have stopped my prayer word; I will return to the loving search." Immediately go back to your prayer. Please notice here that your will has never left the prayer, because you did not consent (an act of the will) to these distractions. It is only when you notice the distractions and deliberately (again, an act of the will) give in to them that your prayer ceases. Begin again until you have passed the allotted time (fifteen or twenty minutes) in this prayer of love. *C P*

CHAPTER 32

• *Which Contains a Plea and Some Instructions about Perseverance*

(See chapter 33 of *The Cloud*)

For God alone my soul waits in silence.

Sometimes, dear friend, nothing seems to work. You try to embrace God in loving prayer and your little house (your mind, remember) is just continuously filled with the chatter, clatter, comings and goings of the little sisters. At these times, you (your will) must just say, "I give up. There is nothing further I can do: I simply leave myself in God's hands."

This is true humility. This is how you stand before God, needing God's help. God will respond. God will come and embrace you. Just try it.

I plead with you, for the love of God, do not give up on your prayer. Start over again every day. Do not look for consolations. Remember again and again that love begins when nothing is expected in return. You will have consolations enough when God wills it. Enjoy them when they are given, but do not look for them or become attached to them. Seek the giver, not the gifts.

Indeed, this is why God allows us to have such problems in our prayer. Usually, it is easy and delightful in the beginning. This is sometimes called the honeymoon period. Everything is a joy. We convince ourselves that we have perfect love, or at least as perfect as can be had in this life.

And then one day, the honeymoon is over. God says, "All right, I drew you to me with sweetness and light. You have tasted and seen that I can be sweet. But there is danger now of your attraction being based on my gifts. I want you to love me for my own sake. I will withdraw, at times, the loving sweetness you have experienced in your prayer so that you can be led to seek me for my own sake. Prove that you love me."

God will seem to withdraw, dear friend, but please realize that God is never so present. Jesus was probably, humanly speaking, never closer to his heavenly Father than when he was perfectly accomplishing his will on the cross. Yet this was the time when he cried out, "My God, My God, why have you abandoned me?" This is how Jesus felt, but what he knew was something quite different. Read on.

CHAPTER 33

• *How Jesus on the Cross Seems to Have Given in to Despair. How True Humility Came to His Rescue*

Do you remember, dear friend, how Jesus cried out to his Father on the cross? "And at the ninth hour Jesus cried out with a loud voice, 'Eloi, Eloi, lama sabach-thani'? which means, 'My God, my God, why hast thou forsaken me?'" (Mk. 15:34). What does this mean? Is it not scandalous? Is Jesus in despair? What about his Father? Has he abandoned him? If he has not, why does he allow it to seem so? If this happened to Jesus, what can we expect? I think we will find it helpful to look into this incident and the questions that flow from it. I am going to share with you now something that is truly fascinating, something that a casual reading of the text in St. Mark's Gospel might not reveal to you.

When St. Mark tells us that on the cross Jesus cried out, "My God, why have you forsaken me," he was doing more, much more, than simply recording words Jesus spoke or telling us that Jesus felt abandoned by God. Scripture scholars bring to our attention that these words are actually a quotation from Psalm 22, verse 1. They also tell us that whenever a verse from the Old Testament is quoted in the New Testament, if we want to know its full meaning, we must go to the Old Testament and read the verses that accompany that verse. The New Testament writer, for brevity's sake, quotes a part of the Old Testament text but assumes that we will know also the accompanying verses.

Here we have something remarkable if we follow this principle. St. Mark is actually telling us that on the cross *Jesus prayed Psalm 22!* St. Mark is not only telling us words that Jesus uttered on the cross (verse 1) but he expects us to realize that Jesus was praying, thinking of, and living out the words of Psalm 22 in its entirety!

CHAPTER 34

· *How Jesus Prayed Psalm 22 on the Cross*

How remarkable this is. Dear friend, we are being told what Jesus was *thinking* when he was being crucified. If we want to know what sentiments, emotions, thoughts, and feelings Jesus had on the cross, all we have to do is read Psalm 22. Do so now. Read (and pray) Psalm 22 with Jesus. Then we shall discuss it.

CHAPTER 35
· *The Mind of Jesus on the Cross,*
Psalm 22

1. My God, My God, why hast thou forsaken me?
   Why art thou so far from helping me,
   From the words of my groaning?
2. O my God, I cry by day, but thou dost not answer,
   And by night, but find no rest.
3. Yet thou art holy,
   Enthroned on the praises of Israel.
4. In thee our fathers trusted;
   They trusted, and thou didst deliver them.
5. To thee they cried, and were saved;
   In thee they trusted, and were not disappointed.
6. But I am a worm, and no man;
   Scorned by men, and despised by the people.
7. All who see me mock at me,
   They make mouths at me, they wag their heads;
8. "He committed his cause to the Lord;
   Let him deliver him,
   Let him rescue him, for he delights in him!"
9. Yet thou art he who took me from the womb;
   Thou didst keep me safe upon my mother's breasts.
10. Upon thee was I cast from my birth,
    And since my mother bore me
    Thou hast been my God.
11. Be not far from me,
    For trouble is near
    And there is none to help.
12. Many bulls encompass me,
    Strong bulls of Bashan surround me;
13. They open wide their mouths at me,
    Like a ravening and roaring lion.
14. I am poured out like water,
    And all my bones are out of joint;

My heart is like wax,
It is melted within my breast;
15. My strength is dried up like a potsherd,
And my tongue cleaves to my jaws;
Thou dost lay me in the dust of death.
16. Yea, dogs are round about me;
A company of evildoers encircle me;
They have pierced my hands and feet—
17. I can count all my bones—
They stare and gloat over me;
18. They divide my garments among them,
And for my raiment they cast lots.
19. But thou, O Lord, be not far off!
O thou my help, hasten to my aid!
20. Deliver my soul from the sword,
My life from the power of the dog!
21. Save me from the mouth of the lion,
My afflicted soul from the horns of the wild oxen!

CHAPTER 36

· Which Continues Psalm 22 but with a Great Difference in Tone, as We Shall See Later

22. I will tell of thy name to my brethren;
In the midst of the congregation, I will praise thee:
23. You who fear the Lord, praise him!
All you sons of Jacob, glorify him,
And stand in awe of him,
All you sons of Israel!
24. For he has not despised or abhorred
The affliction of the afflicted;
And he has not hid his face from him,
But has heard, when he cried to him.
25. From thee comes my praise in the great congregation;
My vows I will pay before those who fear him.

26. The afflicted shall eat and be satisfied;
    Those who seek him shall praise the Lord!
    May your hearts live forever!
27. All the ends of the earth shall remember and turn to
    the Lord;
    And all the families of the nations shall worship
    before him.
28. For dominion belongs to the Lord,
    And he rules over the nations.
29. Yea, to him shall all the proud of the earth bow down,
    Before him shall bow all who go down to the dust,
    And he who cannot keep himself alive.
30. Posterity shall service him;
    Men shall tell of the Lord to the coming generation,
31. And proclaim his deliverance to a people yet unborn
    That He has wrought it.

CHAPTER 37

• *Here Begins an Explanation of
Psalm 22 for Your Encouragement in
Times of Distress in Prayer or in any
Other Thing that May Afflict You in
Your Loving Search*

(See chapter 33 of *The Cloud;* chapters 37 through 51 of
this little book are expansions of chapter 33 of *The
Cloud*)

There you have it, dear friend in God, an intimate, detailed
experience in the mind of Jesus in what was certainly the most
important and difficult moment of his earthly life. But remember
that we are members of the body of Christ and that nothing that
Jesus experienced is foreign to us. Did he not say: "Take up your
cross daily, and follow me"?

It is important for us, then, to take a closer look at this inspired psalm. Let us do it together.

CHAPTER 38

• In which We Seek an Understanding of the First Verses of Psalm 22

> My God, my God, why hast thou forsaken me?
> Why art thou so far from helping me,
> From the words of my groaning?
> O my God, I cry by day, but thou dost not answer,
> And by night, but find no rest.

O my dear friend, what agony is in these words. There is no need for me to repeat in detail what has happened to Jesus to bring him to this state. You know as well as I about his agony in the garden, his arrest, his pseudotrials, his scourging, crowning with thorns, and his journey carrying the cross. You know how he was stripped of his clothes, nailed to the cross, and lifted up for all to see.

Listen to his voice. Hear his agony and despair. Hear how hope has deserted him. But you must listen, dear friend, to more than that. You must hear in the hopelessness and frustration of his voice the cry of the poor, the distressed, the suffering, the ill, the lonely, and the persecuted of every age, even to this present day. And you must hear in the agony of his cry your own voice as you are called to make up in your own life what is wanting in the sufferings of Christ.

Jesus cries by day and by night, but finds no rest, receives no answer. Should we not, at times, have the same experience? But notice that he does not cease to cry out. Even his despair is expressed as a prayer to his Father. And so must we persevere in our trials and in our prayer even when we find no rest.

15 years w/ Hugo
work, child care +
Mom — by God's Grace

5 weeks
2017
X multi cellulitis
main, flu
Aris, GA
- body stiff

CHAPTER 39

· *Jesus Looks to the Temple, the Dwelling Place of His Father*

> Yet thou art holy, enthroned on the praises of Israel.
> In thee our fathers trusted, and thou didst deliver them.
> To thee they cried, and were saved;
> In thee they trusted, and were not disappointed.

As I write these words, dear friend in God, I am only seven miles away from the site of the crucifixion. Often I visit the holy sepulcher, the church that holds under its vast cupola both the sites of the crucifixion and the burial place of Jesus. It is but a ten-minute walk from Golgatha to the temple mount where the magnificent second temple built by Herod stood in all its glory. In its day it was the largest, most magnificent building in the world. There in the holy of holies, the Jews believed, and Jesus acknowledged, God was present. But where was God now?

From his place on Golgatha, Jesus could actually see the temple just a short distance away. The roof over the holy place, with its magnificent columns, could be seen towering over the high walls embracing the temple court. Jesus knew that at that moment there were two hundred thousand Jews from all over the world gathered around Jerusalem for the passover feast. He knew that, at that moment, thousands of them were gathered around and in the temple praying, so that God was literally "enthroned on the praises of Israel."

Thus God has always been with the people. Jesus knew that his ancestors had often called on God in their distress, in Egypt, in the wilderness, in the holy land itself. And God responded. God was always there for them.

But now where was God for Jesus? At the very moment when Jesus breathed his last, St. Mark tells, "And the curtain of the temple was torn in two, from top to bottom." He is talking about the heavy curtain that separated the holy place with its altar of sacrifice from the holy of holies where God had been "enthroned upon the praises of Israel." Horror of horrors! God was no longer there. Not only had Jesus been abandoned, but the entire people of God with him. There seemed to be nothing, only death.

Have not we, you and I, dear friend, been in that position? Let us continue to accompany Jesus through Psalm 22.

CHAPTER 40

* *In which Jesus Sees and Hears the Revilings of the Passers-by, the Priests, the Scribes, and Even the Thieves Crucified with Him. A Warning to Certain Readers.*

> But I am a worm, and no man;
> Scorned by men, and despised by the people.
> All who see me mock at me,
> They make mouths at me, they wag their heads;
> "He committed his cause to the Lord;
> Let him deliver him,
> Let him rescue him, for he delights in him!"

I must give a warning here, dear friend in God, to certain people who tend to fall into what someone has called "worm theology." These are people who are always, in some way or other, unhappy. Perhaps somewhere in their childhood they were told they were no good. Perhaps they were constantly criticized, corrected, and made to feel inferior until they finally internalized this criticism and were incapable of seeing themselves in any other terms than "I am a worm and no man (woman)." My heart goes out to them, but they must take heed lest they use these sentiments of Jesus on the cross as permission to give themselves to self-pity.

Jesus is not wallowing in self-pity. He is acknowledging the treatment he has received as a result of giving himself to the perfect accomplishment of his Father's will. At the same time, he is iden-

tifying with an Old Testament figure given in Isaiah as a forecast
of the messiah:

> He was despised and rejected by men;
> A man of sorrows, and acquainted with grief;
> And as one from whom men hide their faces
> He was despised, and we esteemed him not.
> Surely he has borne our griefs
> And carried our sorrows;
> Yet we esteemed him stricken,
> Smitten by God, and afflicted.
> But he was wounded for our transgressions,
> He was bruised for our iniquities;
> Upon him was the chastisement that made us whole,
> And with his stripes we are healed. [Is. 53]

CHAPTER 41

• *In which We See through the Eyes of Jesus*

See what is happening here, dear friend in God, through the eyes
of Jesus as he looks about himself. Is this what he receives for his
obedience to his Father? Just five days ago he entered Jerusalem in
a joyful procession of admirers proclaiming him as son of David.
And now:

> It was the will of the Lord to bruise him;
> He has put him to grief . . .
> By his knowledge shall the righteous one, my servant,
> Make many to be accounted righteous;
> And he shall bear their iniquities.
> [Is. 53]

Somehow Jesus was aware, even in his despair, that his suffering
was of value. It was the price to be paid because of his love. Had
he not told his disciples, "Greater love has no man than he lay

down his life for his friends." Jesus is the witness of a loving God, that suffering is redemptive.

Yes, dear friend, we are all called to suffer in our own ways, in our own time and places, and according to our own capacities. The loving search does indeed include the way of the cross. We are called to be one with Christ in all things—in his joy—in his labors—in his friendship—in his teachings—in his love and in his sufferings. By seeing these things through the eyes of Jesus, we can unite them to his suffering. By our efforts to receive with love and patience the trials that are imposed on us as we take on our loving search for God, we too become witnesses to God's love, "For just as the sufferings of Christ flow over into our lives, so also through Christ our comfort overflows" (2 Cor. 1:5).

Yes, we can cry out to God. Yes, we can make the words of Psalm 22 our own. Yes, we can unite our trials and sufferings to those of Jesus. We must do this. Are we not all members of the body of Christ? Do we not know that "our old self was crucified with him so that the body of sin might be done away with. Now if we died with Christ, we believe that we shall also live with him" (Rom. 6:8).

"Now you are the body of Christ and each one of you is a part of it." So, dear friend, the cry of Jesus is our cry. The suffering of Jesus is our suffering. And the hope of Jesus, which we shall soon see, is our hope. So, "let the peace of Christ rule in your hearts, since as members of one body you were called to peace. And be thankful" (Col. 3,15).

CHAPTER 42

· *We Are Reminded That Our Blessed*
Lady Had a Special Share in the
Sufferings of Jesus

> Yet thou art he who took me from the womb;
> Thou didst keep me safe upon my mother's breasts,
> Upon thee was I cast from my birth,
> And since my mother bore me thou hast been my God.
> Be not far from me, for trouble is near
> And there is none to help.

I have told you, dear friend in God, that this beautiful Psalm 22 shows us the mind of Jesus on the cross, what he felt and suffered. By now you will have noticed, it also shows you what he saw and heard around him. We have, in the psalm, the extraordinary privilege of entering into the mind, heart, and even the body of Jesus. Are we not, after all, members of the body of Christ? We are actually given to see, as it were, through the half-opened eyes of our dear Savior, through the sweat and blood obscuring them, the soldiers before the cross and his mother at a little distance.

Would it be too much to imagine, dear friend in God, that at this point Jesus looked up and saw his mother, who, St. John tells us, was "standing near the cross of Jesus?" Is there anyone who would not weep together with them? Is this not the risk of love? Its pain as well as its glory? Does it not call us to reach out in compassion to all who mourn, to all who must stand by and see their loved ones suffer, to those who wait by hospital beds, in prison visiting rooms, to those who watch their sons and daughters die in useless wars, who see their children starved to death in a world of plenty?

Jesus reminds his Father that he has been under God's protection since before he was born. Until this point he has felt this protection, known this strength, and has been upheld by this support. But where is it now? His mother is standing near the cross. This simply increases his suffering. Where is God, his heavenly Father? "Be not far from me . . . there is none to help."

Do you see here, dear friend, a change in the cry of Jesus? It seems to me he has gone from despair, "Why have you abandoned me?," to an agonized plea that knows at least that there may be some possibility of a response. "Be not far from me." Could it be that already his Father begins to respond to his prayer?

CHAPTER 43

• *Jesus is Aware of His Surroundings but Perhaps Not at This Moment. The Value of His Suffering*

> I am poured out like water,
> And all my bones are out of joint;
> My heart is like wax,
> It is melted within my breast;
> My strength is dried up like a potsherd,
> And my tongue cleaves to my jaws;
> Thou dost lay me in the dust of death.

O, my dear friend, can this be that same voice that "twists the oaks, and strips the forest bare" (Ps. 29:9), the voice that "thunders from the heavens" (Ps. 18)? Have we not read that "the voice of the Lord is powerful, the voice of the Lord is majestic. The voice of the Lord breaks the cedars" (Ps. 29)? Yet here we hear the voice of Jesus, barely able to utter his cry of anguish; his tongue cleaves to his jaws and he is laid in the dust of death.

Do we not feel this at times, dear friend? That we are weak, ineffectual, useless, our strength dried up? I think you can identify with this sentiment of Jesus as I can. But let me remind you that this *is* the voice of the Lord, powerful and majestic, even in its weakness. Jesus too shared in our loving search. Read on!

CHAPTER 44

· *Jesus Sees the Cruel Response of His Executioners*

> Yea, dogs are round about me;
> A company of evildoers encircle me;
> They have pierced my hands and feet—
> I can count all my bones—
> They stare and gloat over me;
> They divide my garments among them,
> And for my raiment they cast lots.

Do you see how Jesus was particularly aware of the details of his passion? Nothing was spared him. He saw the soldiers gamble for his clothing; he was very much aware of the painful wounds in his hands and feet. We are so used to seeing the crucifixion from the point of view of "outsiders." The four gospels describe the passion of Jesus as seen and interpreted by observers. Psalm 22 gives us the passion of Jesus from "inside," as it were. We hear Jesus himself tell how he felt and what he saw. Truly we can identify with him as he bares our griefs and carries our sorrows.

CHAPTER 45

· *In which We See How Jesus' Prayer Changed from One of Hopelessness to one of Expectation*

> But thou, O Lord, be not far off!
> O thou my help, hasten to my aid!
> Deliver my soul from the sword,
> My life from the power of the dog!
> Save me from the mouth of the lion,
> My afflicted soul from the horns of the wild oxen!

What is Jesus asking for here? How did he expect his soul to be delivered from the sword, his life from the dog, the lion's mouth, and the ox's horns? Did he really expect to have his life spared? Or was he praying for something greater, something that perhaps even he was not quite sure of? Is this a step in the process of his loving search?

This is our movement toward God, dear friend, whether through mental or physical sufferings, through external forces, bodily ills, or through the apparent emptiness, at times, of the arms of our soul when they reach out in contemplative prayer to embrace the God of love and seem to close on emptiness. Remember when Jesus told the apostles, "You know the way, to the place where I am going" (Jn. 14:4). It's true, we do know the way. We must take up our cross daily and follow Jesus. Psalm 22 tells us the way Jesus took.

Without getting too confusing here, dear friend in God, it does seem that part of our way is losing our way. I think Jesus was in this situation at this point. He did what we must do. He gave himself completely to the mercy of God, not knowing or even able to imagine what he needed, except, in some way, to be saved, to be delivered. Misery was so great that he was not able even to imagine what that salvation would consist in. This had to be left in his Father's hands. Have we not been in this position? Is it not a part of the loving search?

CHAPTER 46

• In which We See Something Truly Extraordinary

I will tell of thy name to my brethren;
In the midst of the congregation I will praise thee.
You who fear the Lord, praise him!
All you sons of Jacob, glorify him,
And stand in awe of him, all you sons of Israel!
For he has not despised or abhorred
The affliction of the afflicted;

And he has not hid his face from him,
But has heard, when he cried to him.

But what is this, dear friend? What has happened? Is this still
Jesus on the cross? Could this possibly be his sentiments after what
we have just heard from him?

Do you know what alcoholics say who follow the Twelve Steps
Program as a directive in their loving search? "To move upwards,
you sometimes have to hit bottom first." This is because when you
hit bottom, there is no way to go but up! They have been there
(have you?). They know what Jesus experienced (do we?).

Jesus hit bottom. He could not be in a more wretched, more
miserable, position. His soul was laid down in the dust of death,
his heart was like melted wax, his strength depleted. What did he
do? He threw himself on the mercy of his Father even though he
did not experience his presence or support.

Do you see the way now, dear friend? We must work as though
everything depended on us and pray as though everything depended on God. However, we must also realize that there will be
times when we can do absolutely nothing in terms of our own
work. We will be as helpless as Jesus was on the cross. We will hit
bottom and have no recourse but to cry out to our Father.

But see what happens. As with Jesus, he will not hide his face;
he will hear when we cry to him! When Jesus says he will tell his
name to his brothers in the midst of the congregation, he is actually
referring to the gathering of his local community—perhaps the
synagogue in Nazareth or Caparnaum where he was accustomed
to address those gathered for Sabbath worship. The Lord-fearers
were the gentiles who associated themselves with synagogue worship without actually becoming Jews. Sons of Jacob and Israel were
the Jews, priests, and people who made up the congregation.

Jesus is saying (remember he is still on the cross) that God has
answered his prayer and he will tell God's praises to all his friends
in the midst of the congregation. How can he say this? How can
he claim that God has heard him?

CHAPTER 47

• In which We See the Change Wrought in Jesus on the Cross

Remember, dear friend, that we are being privileged to see the passion of Jesus, not as outside observers, but from within Jesus' mind and heart. Outside observers, at this point, would see no change. They would only see a man in the throes of death. But we who read Psalm 22 realize that something extraordinary has happened. Jesus no longer is in despair. He has actually experienced his Father's response to his prayers. Even though, to the external observer, nothing has happened; Jesus has been touched in his inmost being and given comfort and divine assurance. His experience was not a physical one. He still suffers the physical horrors of the crucifixion but it is now different. He even rejoices at the goodness of his Father and promises to praise him publicly.

Have you had this experience, dear friend in God? If not, I am sure you have seen it in others. They may be afflicted by some terrible disease; they may be dying from it or they may be afflicted by some family issue or some special problem that seems insurmountable. They pray to the Father in their loving search without seeing any solution. In fact there seems to be none offered. Yet somehow they are changed. Their hearts are touched and they are transformed. Let us return to Jesus.

— treasure! mom's softness —
neediness
— hit bottom? Can she be
brave in Christ?

CHAPTER 48

• *Jesus Grows in Grace and Wisdom*

> From thee comes my praise in the great congregation;
> My vows I will pay before those who fear him.
> The afflicted shall eat and be satisfied;
> Those who seek him shall praise the Lord!
> May your hearts live forever!

When Jesus was a child and his parents found him in the temple questioning the wise men, St. Luke tells us that he returned to Nazareth with them and that he grew in age, wisdom, and grace before God and humankind. I believe, dear friend, that he continued to grow in age, wisdom, and grace until he died on the cross. Indeed, why should he have stopped earlier? What is the loving search if it is not a growth in age, wisdom, and grace? Jesus continued the loving search until he breathed his last and successfully concluded it.

We can observe a further step here in Psalm 22. Now Jesus says he will praise the Father in the great congregation. He no longer refers to his local synagogue (congregation) but to the temple itself—the very building he can see from the cross where tens of thousands were gathered at that moment to praise God.

"My vows I will pay," when originally written in Psalm 22 by its Old Testament author, referred to a promise he had made to God to offer a sacrificial animal, usually a lamb, in the temple as an act of thanks. Then he would share the flesh of that animal with the poor who were always present hoping for such a gift from the wealthier Jews. There was even a sort of dining room or "fellowship hall" in the temple area for such sharing, according to some scholars.

When Jesus prayed this psalm, however, we can see a much deeper meaning. "The afflicted (poor) shall eat and be satisfied" now refers to the faithful Christians sacramentally uniting themselves to Christ and to one another by receiving the Eucharist, by sharing in the sacrificial banquet of the lamb of God. He even offers a little prayer in this behalf: "May your hearts live forever!" He is talking about us, dear friend in God, you and me.

CHAPTER 49

· *In which the Loving Praise of the Crucified Jesus Continues to Expand*

> All the ends of the earth shall remember
> And turn to the Lord;
> And all the families of the nations
> Shall worship before him.
> For dominion belongs to the Lord,
> And he rules over the nations.

There seems to be no end to the expansion of the grateful heart of Jesus as he shares it with us in these verses of Psalm 22. Jesus began by praising God in the local congregation; then he went to the great congregation. Thus he says that he will praise his Father in the midst of all his own people, the Jews. But now he goes even further, indeed, to the ends of the earth. His praise will not be limited to the Jews but will be so great that it will even attract the gentiles (the nations) to God—all the families of the nations! Remember, dear friend, that this sentiment was experienced by Jesus on the cross just a short time after he had "hit bottom."

CHAPTER 50

· *In which the Heart of Jesus Expands Even beyond the Ends of the Earth*

> Yea, to him shall all the proud of the earth bow down;
> Before him shall bow all who go down to the dust,
> And he who cannot keep himself alive.

What now, dear friend in God? Where can Jesus go once he has reached the ends of the earth? Where else is there? Jesus is nearing the end of his loving search. His love and his union with the Father is so great that it has burst through the limitations that mere physical sufferings and the threat of death could impose.

He now goes beyond earthly limits and praises God in the abode of the dead. Even the dead shall bow down to his Father. Those who cannot keep themselves alive will live because of Jesus' resurrection. He will die for their sins and rise for their justification, and the dead shall praise God. Do you see now, dear friend, where our loving search will lead us? Union with God in love will never end. The limitations of the ends of the earth will be no barrier for us. Today is the beginning of our eternity.

CHAPTER 51

· *In which the Heart of Jesus Expands Even to the Future*

> Posterity shall serve him;
> Men shall tell of the Lord to the coming generation,
> And proclaim his deliverance to a people yet unborn,
> That he has wrought it.

Now you might say, dear friend, we have reached the end. Where can Jesus go to praise his Father once he has brought those praises to the dead? Ah, but he will leave nothing out. His desire to praise God for goodness (and remember, he is still on the cross) becomes so great that he even goes into the future "to proclaim his deliverance to a people yet unborn." Here is the lordship of Jesus "at whose name every knee should bow, in heaven and on earth and under the earth, and every tongue confess that Jesus Christ is lord, to the glory of God the Father."

How truly we are led to know what the loving search is and where it will lead us. It will include the cross, yes, but it will go far beyond it. Union with God in love *is* the kingdom. "Seek first the kingdom of God and all else shall be given to you."

We have seen how Jesus went from despair, from degradation, from suffering, and from a sense of total failure, to praise and thanksgiving. Not only before his friends, his country, the ends of the world, the dead, but even to the future. This is our destiny, dear friend, our cross and our victory. Jesus has gone before us and invites us to follow him. And now we have a prayer to accompany us. Make Psalm 22 your own prayer even as you make the sentiments, the suffering, the praises, the death, and the resurrection of Jesus your own. Jesus is lord!

CHAPTER 52

• *Which Discusses Methods of Contemplation*

(See chapter 34 of *The Cloud*)

There are, dear friend, many methods of contemplation. By this I mean that there are many approaches by which we can dispose ourselves to the graces of contemplative prayer, of union with God in love. So, in that sense, there really are no methods at all. God must reach out to us and embrace us with loving grace if we are to be united to God in love. Love is a free gift of God. Loving union and even the beginnings of the loving search come from God and from God alone.

When I speak of a method of contemplation, this is what I mean. So let us do away with quibbling and vain and useless arguments for or against the use of methods. They are or they are not useful to dispose us to God's grace. Make your own decision and be at peace and leave others at peace in their decisions.

Be concerned only with this. Do you want to love God? This is a simple question to answer. Sometimes people are concerned as to whether they really do love God and consequently as to whether they are called to the prayer of this loving search. You may not be able to say with certainty that you do love God but you can say with certainty that you *want* to love God. Then that will suffice. This desire comes from God and is a certain sign that God loves you and calls you to love.

CHAPTER 53

• How the Intellect, Memory, and Imagination Must Be Honored by Reading, Meditating, and Praying

(See chapter 35 of *The Cloud*)

We would do well, dear friend, to backtrack a little here and give some attention to three of the ladies who live in our little house (our mind). I have been concentrating on Miss Will and her loving embrace of God in the silence and darkness of her chamber. I would like to remind you again that our other powers, Miss Intellect, Miss Memory, and Miss Imagination, should not be neglected. It is true we do not use them in the contemplative embrace of our loving search—except, perhaps, in our prayer word—but that is minimal. In fact, at that time, we even try to silence them. But these three do have a very important role to play if our prayer of loving is to be genuine. You have heard it said, "To know God is to love God," and "Knowledge precedes love." If we are to love God, we must seek to know God. But to know God, we have to go to the sources where God is revealed. These are teachings of the church, the scriptures, and the reflections on the scriptures by saints and scholars.

We do have to read the scriptures. We do have to read spiritual books and reflect on them. And we do have to take to God in prayer what we learn from them about God and about ourselves.

Just consider the way we looked at Psalm 22. This involved the use of our memory, imagination, and intellect. It included reading, thinking, and praying. By praying here I mean that kind of prayer (often called discursive meditation as distinct from contemplative meditation), which uses the intellect to have a dialogue with God. We simply speak to God in prayer about what we have learned. We do this also with the aid of written prayers, the rosary, the stations of the cross, and similar devotions. We learn about God through our personal studies, our scripture readings, the readings of the liturgy in church, the homilies, and our discussion about these things with others.

All of these things, dear friend in God, lead us to love God more. That means they all contribute to the picture of our loving embrace of God in our contemplative meditation. They should never be neglected, even though the time we spend on them will vary depending upon the graces we receive and the invitation to be at peace and still, loving God in contemplative prayer.

CHAPTER 54
· *How Contemplative Meditation Differs from Other Forms of Prayer*
(See chapter 36 of *The Cloud*)

By now, of course, you realize that the contemplative prayer of the loving search for God differs from these forms of prayer. In the prayer of loving union, we do not use the intellect, the memory, or the imagination. It is enough to focus your attention on your prayer word as an expression of your love. Even here, dear friend, you do not try to analyze the prayer word for its meaning or its associations in your past. Seek to experience immediately the love it symbolizes through the loving attention of your will.

As a general rule, I would advise you to keep the same prayer word all the time. However, we cannot find God with our rules.

There may be times when his love can be better symbolized by another prayer word or by no word at all. Just give yourself to God by whatever way God calls you. I remember well a novice telling me that for the better part of a year, he could only sit before the tabernacle in silence, conscious of his need for God. There were no words, no feelings of love, only need.

Let me tell you, dear friend, this was contemplative prayer of the highest level. That need came from God. It was God calling the novice to the loving search and even revealing Godself to him as the object of that search. May God's name be praised!

CHAPTER 55

• How Contemplative Meditation Leads to the Contemplative Attitude

It does not take long, dear friend in God, before you will start to notice that your contemplative meditation spills over, as it were, into the other activities of your daily life. It enters into your other forms of prayer, making them more spontaneous. It enlightens your meditations on the scriptures or church teachings or your own life in pursuit of the virtues. It enters into your recited prayers such as the psalms or the prayers of the liturgy, transforming them, bringing them to a new level of understanding.

It is not limited to your prayer activity. The love of God, which you specifically focus on in the special prayer of your loving search, begins to permeate all of your activities, even the most prosaic. "Whether you eat or drink, or whatever you do, you do it all for the glory of God" (1 Cor. 10:31).

At first perhaps you will not notice this, so subtle are the workings of God. It is not unlikely that others will notice it in you before you do yourself. It does not matter. The love of God will do its work in transforming you.

CHAPTER 56

• *Why We Should be Able to*
Understand How the Prayer
of Our Loving Search Touches the Heart
of God

(See chapter 38 of *The Cloud*)

[handwritten margin notes: Wow. full of purpose to be in union w/ us.]

I do not quite know how to say this, dear friend in God, because
we do not have a language adequate to express it. When you sum
up, as it were, the totality of your love for God in a simple prayer
word, that word is empowered by the Holy Spirit. It directly
pierces the heavens; it goes right to the heart of God. That word,
through the love it symbolizes, is given to you by God and it must
return to him.

> As the rain and the snow come down from heaven, and
> do not return to it without watering the earth and making
> it bud and flourish, so that it yields seed for the sower
> and bread for the eater, so is my word that goes out from
> my mouth. It will not return to me empty, but I will
> accomplish what I desire and achieve the purpose for
> which I sent it. (Isaias 55, 10–11)

Can you see why, dear friend, this prayer of loving union is
so effective?

Even we, as sinful as we are, love those who love us. Or, at the
very least, we are well disposed toward them. It is hardly likely
that we would refuse to respond to their needs, especially for something easily within our power. In the same way, we can expect
God to respond to our needs, to answer our prayers. We love God
because God first loved us and empowers our love. Could God
ignore the cry of that love?

[handwritten note at bottom: He / We can't love on our own even be on our own. He is our Source of Being.]

Thru our weakness God loves us + pardons us!

CHAPTER 57

· *Which Treats of How Much We Should Love God*

(See chapter 41 of *The Cloud*)

I remember as a child being asked how much Jesus loved me. The answer I was taught to give was to stretch my arms out full length (hence, in the form of a cross) and say, "This much!" But how much am *I* to love God?

Jesus answered that one. He simply repeated the words of his Father as found in the Old Testament. "Love the Lord your God with all your heart and with all your soul and with all your strength" (Dt.6:5 and Mt. 22:37). We have been told that virtue stands in the middle, that moderation should be practiced in all things. In general this is true. In fact the physical and mental health that moderation brings about is even necessary in order to love God as we should—unless at times God allows us to be weak, as Jesus was on the cross, as a special way to lead us on the loving search.

St. Bernard of Clairvaux, the great father of the Cistercian Order, was once asked by a friend what should be the measure of her love for God. His reply was, "The measure of your love for God should be to love without measure."

How do we translate this in our lives in terms of the time we spend engaged in the prayer of loving union with God? I hesitate to put time limits on this prayer. But we must deal with ourselves with an awareness of our human limitations.

I would like to suggest as an ideal that you give yourself to the prayer of love twice a day for fifteen to twenty minutes each time. This is an ideal. It is not a requirement. Indeed for many people it is impossible. Then I would suggest once a day for fifteen to twenty minutes as you have the time and opportunity. If this does not work for you, I would suggest once or twice a week, or even simply whenever you feel the call to go apart and express your love for God by gently offering God the symbol of your love in your prayer word.

I would not like to see this as something you must do, but rather as something you want to do. You know how to do it. You know why you should do it. Do not let it become just another thing you neglect and then have guilt feelings for that neglect. Love God with your heart, soul, and strength. Start over again every day!

CHAPTER 58

• *How Contemplative Meditation Can Overflow into Your Daily Habits*
(See chapter 42 of *The Cloud*)

Jesus said of Mary Magdalene that she loved much, therefore much was forgiven her. Love, dear friend, transforms. It transforms idle into industrious, lazy into vigorous, timid into courageous, sinners into saints. It will influence every area of your life.

As I write this, I find myself saying, "Wait a minute! You don't want it to sound as if love is the answer to everything, as if love would solve all of life's problems, as if you could just love and do what you want." On reflection, dear friend in God, I *do* want to sound that way. The human problem, social or personal, has never existed that could not be solved by love.

I do not think that this is a matter of argument. It can only be a matter of experience. It can only be proven by loving. See how it will change your life. See how it will teach you how to respond to the thousand and one daily decisions you must make. Things will assume their proper proportions, even such mundane items as sleeping, eating, and drinking.

Love of God will prompt you to a responsible regimen of spiritual reading, liturgical prayer, and devotional commitments. Love of neighbor will call you to a generous giving of yourself and your material goods in service. Love of self will inspire you to care for your own physical and mental well-being in a way that will be neither excessive nor neglectful. You will always find God when and where you need God, because you will always be united to God in love. God will say to you, "Before you call upon me, I say to you, here I am" (Is. 59, 8).

Before a word is on my lips, God has heard it in my thoughts — his eagerness to love me! + respond to me + you!

CHAPTER 59

◆ *What Stands between You and God*

(See chapter 43 of *The Cloud*)

I know this will sound strange to you, dear friend, but believe me, I know it to be true. The greatest obstacle between you and God in your loving prayer is yourself. In comparison with this obstacle, everything else is a breeze. In your loving prayer it is relatively easy to get rid of exterior obstacles. By closing your eyes, you eliminate the obstacles of sight and most of the exterior world. By sitting quietly in a more or less comfortable (but not too comfortable) chair with your feet flat on the floor, you eliminate the obstacles of feeling. By seeking a relatively quiet place where interruptions will be minimal, you eliminate obstacles of hearing. Taste and smell of themselves present little in the way of interfering with prayer. Later, I will treat of the five senses more completely but, annoying as they can be, they are not major obstacles.

You, my friend, are the major obstacle, and the worst noises are the noises from within. If you want to be a true lover of God, you must love God even more than you love yourself. As St. John the Baptist said of Jesus, "He must increase, I must decrease." This is not easy to say and to really mean.

Remember when we read Psalm 22 and listened to the interior sentiments of Jesus on the cross. What he experienced there, and what we must experience also in our own ways and with our own crosses, is the complete emptying of self. Often it is only by such suffering, only by our souls being "laid down in the dust of death," that we are brought to that perfect love where we can say, along with St. Paul, "I live now, not I, but Christ lives in me."

I AM becomes we are.

* *false self then surrendered to true self in divine union*

CHAPTER 60

· *In which We Begin to See How the Obstacle of Self Is Removed by God*
(See chapter 44 of *The Cloud*)

Does this frighten you, dear friend in God? Perhaps it should. Yet, at the same time it must be said that love can make it easy, and perfect love can make it a joy. Do you recall how, in Psalm 22, we saw Jesus go from suffering and despair to joy and resplendent praise of God?

We do not make a long journey in a single step. The loving search is made step by step on a daily basis. We need not be overconcerned with what we meet on the way. God is with us; God began the journey for us and waits for us at the end.

It is good for us to be aware of the extent to which we are separated from God. This is what calls us to seek greater union. But this awareness should never be allowed to discourage us. We should regret it, yes, even weep because of it. Sometimes we may even find ourselves crying out with Jesus, "My God, why have you abandoned me?" But always we should remember and cling to the hope it brings us, that Jesus made the journey before us and shows us the way. He said, "I am the way."

So be patient. Do not try for short cuts or run to people or even religions that promise you sudden and extraordinary religious experiences. The world abounds with them today. Rely on the guidance of the church, on prayer, and on good, proven advice.

CHAPTER 61

· How God Is Pleased When We Are as Little Children

(See chapter 46 of *The Cloud*)

Dear friend, when it comes to contemplative prayer, we should be more like little children playing at the feet of their father than like soldiers trying to storm a fortress. Remember that St. Paul tells us that "love is patient, love is kind. It does not envy, it does not boast, it is not proud. It is not rude, it is not self-seeking, it is not easily angered" (1 Cor. 13:4f.). He could have also added that love does not force; it does not use pressure; it is not demanding.

In our loving search for union with God in contemplative prayer, we will accomplish more by a joyful enthusiasm than by a demanding, forceful effort. Even humanly speaking, we would get a better response by entering someone's presence in a peaceful, quiet way, showing eager joy, than by forcing our way in by determined effort and compulsive drive.

God will love you better when you approach God with the gentle simplicity of a child. God will bend over and take you to heart.

CHAPTER 62

· In which We Consider the Place of Emotions in Our Loving Search

(See chapters 47 and 48 of *The Cloud*)

We are, dear friend, neither spiritual nor physical beings but a combination of both. Therefore, you will not be surprised when I say that our loving search must have physical as well as spiritual elements. Our emotions are really a product of our physical side. By themselves, they are suspect, but when balanced by a mature understanding, they are truly human activities that have a great part to play in our loving search.

Externally motivated enthusiasm is not from God. It may be good and useful or it may be evil, but it is not spiritual. I am sorry to say that we see a great deal of this kind of enthusiasm today passing off for religion. Television seems to be a popular medium for this kind of hype. Beware of emotional responses generated by overenthusiastic "Bible thumping" preachers or by media-generated audience enthusiasm, stimulated by stage effects and electronic embellishments.

I remember, one Sunday morning in a hotel, turning on the television before going out to celebrate Mass. It was a "religious" program conducted by a popular televangelist. All the standard props were used; a large choir electronically enhanced, a stage filled with flowers, attractive women modestly but expensively clothed, and an overenthusiastic preacher who strode back and forth across the stage waving his Bible. I quickly became absorbed in the theatrics and found myself emotionally responding to the enthusiasm of the preacher and his audience. It took a few minutes before the horror of his message penetrated through to my critical understanding. With all the panoply of "popular" religion, choir, Bibles, church robes, and the like, the man was extolling the amassing of money and material goods as a sign of God's favor and promising them to his audience in great abundance, if they would donate heavily to his ministry!

You see, dear friend in God, I was momentarily lost in the externals. My emotions were responding, but not my mind. Many were and are taken in by this ersatz religion. The man had before him a large audience and, in addition, a television following. There was nothing in his person or his message that truly related to the loving search.

The fruits of the Spirit show us the true use and value of emotions. They come from within, from a heart touched by God. They are "love, joy, peace, patience, kindness, goodness, faithfulness, gentleness, and self-control. Against such things there is no law. Those who belong to Christ Jesus have crucified the sinful nature with its passions and desires" (Gal. 5:23–24).

Christ died + made power of sin impotent! dead ... I choose to live in new power He released in his resurrection ... we are victorious! (CP, CP Lectio lifestyle)

overstating ... hatred of flesh

CHAPTER 63

• *Which Makes Some Observations on the Gift of Tongues*

(See chapter 48 of *The Cloud*)

I think, dear friend in God, that it is appropriate here to make some observations regarding the gift of tongues. As we see it today, this gift is probably the same one mentioned in the letters of St. Paul and especially in 1 Corinthians, chapters 12 to 14. However, we must make some distinctions here. The speaking of the apostles to the people on Pentecost was not the gift of tongues as we understand it today. That was clearly a miraculous phenomenon. The people then present spoke any one of fifteen languages (Acts 2) and each heard the apostles speak in his or her own particular language.

In 1 Corinthians, St. Paul is speaking of something quite different. In fact, he says, "One who speaks in a tongue speaks not to men but to God; for no one understands him" (1 Cor. 14:2), and again, "If you in a tongue utter speech that is not intelligible, how will anyone know what is said? For you will be speaking into the air." And again, "In church I would rather speak five words with my mind, in order to instruct others, than ten thousand words in a tongue." He then goes on to tell his readers not to allow tongues in the church except for two or at the most three persons, and then only one at a time and with someone to interpret. If there is no one to interpret, he says, "let each of them keep silence in church and speak to himself and to God" (1 Cor. 14:27f.).

CHAPTER 64

• *In Defense of the Gift of Tongues*

Now, dear friends, I am familiar, firsthand, with the gift of tongues. I have been associated with charismatic prayer groups since they first appeared in Catholic communities in the 1960s. I have assisted in organizing such groups and have been spiritual adviser to them, as well as to many individuals in them. I have celebrated the Eucharist regularly with a charismatic group of three to four hundred people. After communion it was the custom for us to return to our seats for a period of silent prayer. Gradually we would begin to pray and even to sing in tongues. It was a spontaneous, gentle, joyful expression of praise, quite in accord with St. Paul's instructions, as each, in the context of the community gathering, was praising God, in a real sense, privately.

In other contexts, I have also shared in speaking in tongues with interpretation as St. Paul instructs. This is definitely not a word-for-word interpretation such as, for example, one would interpret German or French for an English-speaking person. Rather it was done with a gentle urging and a sense of correctness. One simply felt that the Holy Spirit was prompting someone to deliver a specific edifying message, inspired by the person who spoke the tongues. As St. Paul advises, "When you come together, each one has a hymn, a lesson, a revelation, a tongue, or an interpretation. Let all things be done for edification" (1 Cor. 14:26).

CHAPTER 65

• A Personal Explanation of the Gift of Tongues

Dear friend, I would like to attempt, for your instruction, to give a personal explanation of the gift of tongues. Let me emphasize that it is personal and you do not have to accept it. If it helps you understand the issue, then I am grateful. If you or someone else has a better explanation, then forget what I have said and accept what suits you. Anything I say is subject to the superior wisdom of the church.

Again let me remind you that tongues, as described in 1 Corinthians by St. Paul, is not a miracle. The phenomenon can be found in many cultures in contexts that have nothing to do with religion. This does not mean that tongues, in a religious context, is not prayer or not supernatural. I believe that it is. But it does not go beyond the laws of nature, which is our traditional understanding of miracles.

We are told by theologians, who know much more about the subject than I do, that the supernatural is based on the natural. By this is meant that the Spirit-graced events of our life, such as the sacraments, prayer, the liturgy are natural activities that are raised to the level of the supernatural by the grace of God. They are not miraculous in their foundations; they are natural. Perhaps some examples will help. The very natural activity of washing with water, when done in a church context in response to grace and with the proper words signifying that intention, becomes the supernatural sacrament of baptism. The very natural activity of eating bread and drinking wine, when done in the eucharistic context, becomes a supernatural act of receiving the body and blood of Christ. Do you see, dear friend, these are not miraculous, but they are supernatural. Their effect on us is also supernatural. We grow in the grace of God. We are changed in a supernatural way

CHAPTER 66

• A Further Example of the Differences between the Supernatural and the Miraculous

Imagine that there are two men standing side by side reciting the Lord's prayer. One of these men is a fervent Christian; the other is an atheist. Naturally speaking, they are doing exactly the same thing. They are both speaking words in a human voice in the normal human way of speaking. They are both mouthing exactly the same words. This is the natural situation of these two men. However, supernaturally, the reality is quite different. The Christian prays. He is speaking to his loving Father. The atheist is simply uttering words. The Christian is not involved in anything miraculous, but he is performing a supernatural act—based on a natural one.

CHAPTER 67

• How This Difference Is Related to the Gift of Tongues through Intellect and Will

Now, dear friend in God, let me relate this to the gift of tongues, as I understand it. Accept or reject it, as you will. Remember the example I have been using of the mind being a little house and its primary occupants being the intellect and the will. It is the business of the intellect to ponder, to think, to reason, to intellectualize. This is a simple, natural function. Recall how she invites passersby (truths) in for tea to question them. Now when the intellect has done some thinking about a certain truth, she often wants to communicate this, especially to the will, but also to other intellects. To do this, she often uses the help of the memory and imagination.

She also, and especially when communicating with others, will make use of the *body!* That is, she will articulate in words the truth she wants to share. She uses, under her intelligent direction, our voice boxes, our throats, our breath, our tongues, and our lips. When in response to the gift of faith, she wants to articulate a truth in speech to God (e.g., to say the Our Father), this natural phenomenon of speech is raised to a supernatural level and she prays. The will also shares in this because it is she who prompts the intellect to pray and who inspires the prayer by way of her supernatural gift of love.

Now what happens when the will has a profound experience of the presence of God and the intellect has gone to sleep (because she cannot express infinite truth)? In the beginning stages of this experience, the will may want to express her joy in the way she is accustomed—that is, through the body, through the voice. But remember now that she cannot, at this time, articulate her experience in intelligent words, because intelligent speech is the work of the intellect, not the will. The intellect is not then functioning.

So what does the will do? She tries to express in speech, using the vocal apparatus, her joy, praise, and love without the help of the intellect. What results is the gift of tongues—a supernatural prayer in which our loving faculty expresses vocally (but not intelligently) her love for God. As St. Paul says, "God has poured out his love into our hearts by the Holy Spirit whom he has given us" (Rom. 5:5), and "the Spirit helps us in our weakness. We do not know [intellect!] what we ought to pray for, but the Spirit himself intercedes for us with groans that words cannot express" (that the intellect cannot express). St. Paul seems to support this explanation also when he says, "If I pray in a tongue, my spirit prays, but my mind is unfruitful" (1 Cor. 14:14).

I hope this is clear to you, dear friend. It seems to me a satisfying explanation of what could otherwise be a very confusing phenomenon.

CHAPTER 68

• *How Tongues Is Probably the First*
Stage of Contemplative Prayer for Some
People

Can you see now why I make the claim that tongues is the first
stage of contemplative prayer? In the contemplative prayer of our
loving search, the will rests quietly, content in the loving embrace
of God without the help of the intellect. But in the beginning of
this experience, when it is new and unfamiliar, the will seeks to
express it bodily as she has been accustomed to do with her other
experiences in which the intellect was active. This is also why I
think the gift of tongues is usually a temporary gift, one that we
often joyfully experience, but then we pass beyond the need for it.
It must also be stressed here that it is not a necessary gift. Many
loving Christians never receive it.

St. Paul tells us that not everybody will speak in tongues, just
as not everyone will be a bishop (administrator), an apostle (an
actual witness of the resurrected Christ), or a prophet (speaker for
God). But, he says, "Earnestly desire the higher gifts. And I will
show a more excellent way. If I speak in the tongues of men and
of angels but have not love, I am a noisy gong or a clanging cym-
bal." Then he goes on to say that love is the greatest gift of all in
what is perhaps the most beautiful passage in the entire Bible
(1 Cor. 13). Love is what we should desire.

CHAPTER 69
• *How the Gift of Tongues Leads to Silence. How Abuses Must Be Avoided*

It has been my experience with tongues, dear friend, both privately and in prayer groups, that it leads to silence. This is a deeper level of the prayer of our loving search. Perhaps you have seen it yourself. A prayer group, in its first few weeks or months, tends to manifest a lot of praying in tongues, often, unfortunately, without the interpretations St. Paul insists on. But then if the members are correctly guided and responsive to the Spirit, periods of silence become more common. These periods consist in a simple loving of God in contemplative silence.

CHAPTER 70
• *A Warning about Some So-Called Charismatics or Pentecostals Who Are Ignorant of Contemplative Prayer*

I do feel here, dear friend, that the truth requires that I issue a warning. There are some, even priests and nuns, but especially people who come from non-Catholic traditions, who do not understand contemplative prayer, and who are even afraid of it. They think that you are not praying unless you are externally active. There must be handwaving or singing or tongues or Bible readings or sermons constantly going on. Some of these people, in their ignorance (good willed, I will presume), even speak of silent prayer as "the void" and warn of the possibility of the devil's taking over one's mind

Let me say this. I do not know what "the void" is. I do know, as I hope you know also, what it is to love God in the silence and darkness of contemplative love without thoughts or emotional expressions. I do not know any "void." For me everything is filled with the grandeur of God even if I cannot always see it. For God, and for anyone who loves God, there can be no empty place, no void, because God fills all creation.

As for the devil, I do not fear him. Nor can I approve of those who seem to be living a kind of constant "devil theology." It almost seems as if they pay more attention to the devil than to God. They see him behind every telephone pole and under every bed. He seems to play a great role in their lives, as they are always talking about him.

I would rather talk about God and see God where God is—behind every telephone pole and under every bed and everywhere else. Let those who constantly worry about the devil worry about him. Let those who fear some kind of a "void" fear it. As for me, and, I hope, for you, dear friend, I will continue on in the loving search with the help of God's grace and "even though I walk through the valley of the shadow of death, I will fear no evil, for God is with me" (Ps. 23).

CHAPTER 71

• *The Greatest Gift of All, the Attraction toward God*

(See chapter 49 of *The Cloud*)

Dear friend, the greatest gift that God can give you in this world or the next is Godself. What a joy it should be to feel in your inmost heart that little tug of what has been called "the gentle stirring of love." This is God's call, God's offering of self, God's response to your loving search. Indeed, your loving search would not have even begun without this gentle call.

I am sure you know what I mean. It comes as a sudden awareness or as a gentle reminder. It can be at prayer, during recreation, or while waiting for sleep. It is hard to describe. It comes in a variety of ways and awarenesses. Perhaps the best way to describe it as "a gentle stirring of love" and leave it at that.

Do you realize what happens when you respond to God's grace in love? Do you know truly what is going on when you go aside for your fifteen or twenty minutes of loving God in contemplative meditation? You are accomplishing, in the best way possible, the purpose for which you were created—union with God. When you are united to God, you are united to all creation. Nothing is separated from or foreign to you. The past, present, and future are one. In loving God, you love all that God loves—strangers, acquaintances, friends, enemies, the dead. Even those yet unborn and the entire host of angels are one with you in this love. This is truly "where it is." This is truly "what it is all about."

Is it any wonder that Jesus told Martha that there was only one thing necessary, and that Mary had chosen the better part, and he could not take it from her? My friend, when we give ourselves to this love, we lack nothing here or hereafter. "Eye has not seen, nor ear heard, nor has mind conceived what God has prepared for those who love him" (1 Cor. 2:9). In this union with God, as we give ourselves to it more and more, we reach a complete harmony with God's will. We want only what God wants. Like Jesus we become the "Amen" to the Father, seeking and desiring only to fulfill God's will in all things.

In a very real sense, suffering and consolations become the same for us—as long as God wills them. We begin to see things more and more through the eyes of Christ. We experience our oneness with God so completely that it is in God that we live and move and have our being (Acts 17:28).

A will united to God in love partakes by that very fact in the highest perfection. Our sins are forgiven and a promise of future glory is given to us. Of course there yet remains for us to fill up "what is lacking in the sufferings of Christ" (Col. 1:24), but "just as the sufferings of Christ flow over into our lives, so also through Christ our comfort overflows" (2 Cor. 1:5).

CHAPTER 72

• *Consolations Vary from Person to Person, and from Time to Time*
(See chapter 50 of *The Cloud*)

My dear friend in God, love is a joy even though it may be without sensible consolations. When we love God, we want to give ourselves to that love in contemplative meditation whether we receive consolations or not. It seems that some people are being constantly overwhelmed with sensible delights in their meditation, while others receive little or none at all. Perhaps, though, you are like me. Sometimes my contemplative prayer is filled with peace and a simple joy. Other times it seems to be just a kind of rote offering of my will, through my prayer word, amidst constant distractions. But truly it does not matter. There is one thing necessary—to love God.

Often I am asked if contemplative meditation will become easier with time and familiarity. This is hard to answer, because I do not know how God will deal with any given individual. I presume this question concerns distractions, the constant efforts of the memory and the imagination (and sometimes the intellect) to interfere with our silent loving of God. One thing I can say in answer to this question is that you will feel more and more (with practice) that you are able to deal with these things whether they actually lessen in intensity or not.

CHAPTER 73

• *Some Help from St. Thérèse of Lisieux*

God knows when we are in need of consolation. God will give them what divine love dictates. We will not be tested beyond our endurance. I like very much the example St. Thérèse of Lisieux uses to explain her experience in this matter. She says at times she feels like she is under leaden skies. Day after day there are only heavy clouds rolling over her. She begins to forget what the sun was like. She wonders if she ever really felt its warmth, or ever saw its brilliance.

And then suddenly one day, without warning, the clouds part and the sun bursts through, shedding its warmth and light, and she glories in its comfort. There may still be clouds and the sun may be hidden once again, but she is encouraged when she needs it. So does she experience God in her loving search.

CHAPTER 74

• *St. Teresa of Avila Shares the Experience of Her Loving Search*

St. Teresa of Avila uses a different image and a somewhat different approach. It may be useful for some to see it in their own loving search. I leave it up to them. She tells us that God's grace and, to some extent, God's consolations differ as we advance in the loving search. She compares it to watering a garden. She is speaking in terms of the effort that seems to be involved in our loving search for God. I think we are justified in adapting her image for our present purpose.

Our loving search for God can be compared to the four ways of watering a garden that it might bear fruit. The first way, St. Teresa tells us, is that laborious, methodical task of carrying water to the garden with buckets, one by one. This is sometimes how we have to begin our loving search.

The second way is by a waterwheel or a windmill. Here we have a device that brings the water to us, so we do not have to let buckets down the well one by one. We still have to carry them to the garden and water the plants, but it is easier. God makes it simpler for us and the water is more abundant. Dear friend, when I speak here of water, you must understand grace.

The third way, an even simpler and more plentiful way to water the garden, is by irrigation. Now the water runs freely to the garden from an inexhaustible source such as a river. Sometimes we even have to, in a sense, control it so that it does not overwhelm the garden.

The fourth way is the easiest and the best of all. We do not have to do anything. It rains! Now the water comes as a total and complete gift of God. We simply have to be there, open and willing to receive the superabundance of God's love and grace.

CHAPTER 75

· How All These Approaches Apply to Us at Different Times

I think, dear friend in God, you will recognize all these approaches to the loving search. No doubt you have experienced them all, from the cloudy skies of St. Thérèse of Lisieux to the rain of St. Teresa of Avila. It is good to be aware of these variations and to expect them in our own loving searches and in the contemplative meditation that is at the heart of the search. What is most important of all to realize is that whichever situation we may find ourselves in, there is only one thing that matters, and that is to be in loving union with God throughout it all.

CHAPTER 76

• How the Contemplative Experience of the Loving Search Is so Simple and Yet so Difficult to Describe

(See chapter 51 of *The Cloud*)

One thing is certain, dear friend, and that is that you can trust God. Whenever you feel in your heart that gentle stirring of love for God, you do not have to be concerned about where it comes from. You should simply give yourself to it by reaching up to God or reaching within. Actually I am not sure whether I should say "reaching up" to God or "reaching within." Both are true, because God is everywhere. It is simply a matter of your own perceptions and feelings. Some say that when you peacefully and lovingly offer your prayer word in your contemplative meditation, you should see it as gently coming forth from your heart and going up to God in heaven. Others prefer to say that the prayer, that symbol of your love for God, goes deeper into the very center of your being where God dwells.

Both are correct and indeed there are even other ways to visualize or to express your experience of loving God. It is difficult to find words to adequately express the experience of God in our loving search. This is why so many of the great mystics were poets. They realized that the only way they could talk about their experiences was through the language of poetry.

I think, dear friend, we need not be too concerned about how this experience is expressed. To love God is to love God! It is to do the one thing necessary. It is to choose the better part. It is to become truly what we are called to be and what we are. It is to find our spiritual nourishment, our rest and our joy, in the only place where they can authentically be realized, in the heart of God.

Give yourself over gently to the experience of this love. The God of hope will fill you with all joy and peace as you trust in God, so that you may overflow with hope and love by the power of the Holy Spirit (cf. Rom. 15:15).

CHAPTER 77

· How Seldom We Have the Experience of Sitting Still for Twenty Minutes

Do you know, my dear friend in God, that when you give yourself over to twenty minutes of loving God, according to the manner described in this little book, you are doing something quite ordinary and, at the same time, quite unusual. It is quite ordinary, because all of God's children are called to God in love. God loves us all and wants us all to love God in return. This is a grace certainly, but it is a grace that is available to all.

It is quite unusual because this grace is so frequently neglected. In our society we do not seem to have time for God. There are so many activities and distractions available to us that we do not often give the priority to the one thing necessary. Just contrast, if you will, the amount of time you spend watching television and the amount of time you spend in prayer!

I am not saying that you must pray as often as you watch television or give both equal time. What I am saying is that television is simply one of a number of activities that consume our time and that make prayer time hard to find.

I have been suggesting that for the contemplative prayer of this loving search, you should go apart for twenty minutes. During this time you are expected to sit quietly offering your prayer word as a symbol of your love for God. You do nothing else. You do not read, or knit, or watch television; you simply love God in and for Godself, and without any aid except your loving prayer word.

In the scores of workshops and retreats where I have taught this prayer of our loving search to hundreds of people, I often ask them this question after their first experience of contemplative meditation: When was the last time that you sat perfectly still for twenty minutes without a television set in front of you? Many people, unfortunately, will shake their heads and reply: Never!

CHAPTER 78

• *Which Talks about Release Phenomena*

(See chapter 52 of *The Cloud*)

Dear friend, the simple experience of sitting quietly in contemplative prayer for twenty minutes is unusual for our culture. We do not know what to expect from it even in a natural sense, never mind in a supernatural sense. There are some things that we sometimes experience, especially in the beginning of our loving search. I call these things "release phenomena," because they represent tensions that we hold into ourselves through and in the hyper activities of our daily lives. This is true even if we do not consider ourselves to be busy people. Our culture offers us all the distractions and occasions we need to keep these tensions penned up within ourselves. When we give ourselves to contemplative meditation, these tensions are often released in various ways. I do not think we need to be concerned about them, but it is helpful to know what they may be. It is also helpful to know that once released, these tensions are lessened in our persons and we are left with feelings of relaxation, calm, and peace. All of this, of course, further disposes us to experience in our lives the fruits of the Spirit.

These release phenomena can take the form of a prickly feeling in different parts of the body. There can be a loss of sensation in various parts of the body also, but without the uncomfortable sensation we experience when a human limb "falls asleep" and then returns to its normal state. A sudden jerking movement of the arms or legs may startle us for a moment, but is only to be seen as a tension release also. Some people find themselves breaking out in sweat as a release phenomenon.

It is not unusual for some people to have a kind of feeling of fear. This is often expressed by a sensation of falling, or, at least, standing at a great height and fearing a possible fall. This is probably a result of the fact that in this meditation we actually give up the normal control of our intellect. As a result we have the awareness that we are not in total control of ourselves in our accustomed manner. The imagination seeks to express this feeling in some traditional way. I have not known this experience to be extended. It seems to go away after a few meditations. It need not concern us, because we are putting control of ourselves in the loving hands of God, who "will command his angels concerning you to guard you in all your ways; they will lift you up in their hands, so that you will not strike your foot against a stone" (Ps. 91:11).

CHAPTER 79
· *Which Begins to Describe Some of the Fruits of the Contemplative Meditation of Your Loving Search for God*
(See chapter 54 of *The Cloud*)

Dear friend, I have told you repeatedly that this loving prayer is done for its own sake. We need no further motive for loving God than loving God. We love God for God's own sake, because God is worth loving. I have also told you that love begins when nothing is expected in return. Why then am I now proposing to tell you about the fruits of loving God?

I must do this, dear friend, because God will not be outdone in generosity. There is no limit to God's kindness. In this prayer God gives us Godself. That is our main concern. However, God also gives us many lesser gifts. We would do well to look at some of these.

Jesus told his disciples, "Come apart with me to a quiet place and rest" (Mt. 6:31). God also said, "Come to me, all you who are weary and burdened, and I will give you rest" (Mt. 11:28). You probably know by now, dear friend, that contemplative meditation is restful. It reenergizes. God creates in us a new heart and a steadfast spirit (Ps. 51); God gives us the Spirit for our recreation (Ps. 104:30). This is perhaps the most common and most consistent gift of our loving search for God.

This is even a reason why I urge people to meditate when they are tired in a healthy way—that is, after some physical work or exercise, or toward the end of the morning or the afternoon. Our physical bodies are usually somewhat tired at those times. They are not apt to disturb our meditation by fidgeting or wanting action. But also by our contemplative meditation, we rest in God's love and receive the restoration we need.

CHAPTER 80

• *Contemplation Results in a Lessening of Body Tensions*

Another fruit of this loving prayer, dear friend, is a lessening of body tensions. Actual tests taken have shown that people with high blood pressure are greatly helped. There is also a calming effect experienced especially in areas where you might be worried or anxious or fearful. This is to be expected when we realize that in this prayer God pours out God's love into our hearts by the Holy Spirit who is given to us (Rom. 5:5) and that the fruits of the Spirit are love, joy, peace, patience, kindness, goodness, faithfulness, gentleness, and self-control (Gal. 5:23).

God wants us to have these gifts and it is all right for us to expect them and rejoice in them. God wants us to live by the Spirit and to keep in step with God (Gal. 5:24).

CHAPTER 81

• *As We Resemble Christ More and More, We Put on the Mind of Christ*

(See chapter 54 of *The Cloud*)

St. Paul says, "We have the mind of Christ" (1 Cor. 2:16). You see, dear friend, those who love Christ and who resemble him, greatly aided by this prayer of our loving search, come more and more to see the world and all it holds through the eyes of Christ. This is true wisdom, to know God's creation as Christ knows it. Indeed who could know it better? "He was in the beginning, with

God; all things were made through him and without him was not anything made that was made" (Jn. 1:2).

Perhaps, most important of all, we are led by this loving prayer to know ourselves as we truly are and even as we would be without the grace of God. This is true humility. Our decisions and our actions become more Christlike "because Christ's love compels us" (1 Cor. 5:14). We gradually sense in our own lives a growth in patience, kindness, forgiveness, and trust (1 Cor. 13). We even begin to radiate this Christlikeness in our lives in such a way that others are affected by it and attracted to Christ.

CHAPTER 82

• The Loving Search Changes Us Spiritually and Even Physically

The love of God, dear friend, as we have seen, changes us from within. Is it not to be expected then that those changes will be observable from without? I think we have all seen this in some elderly people. It may be that they are not beautiful by normal human standards, but the sense of God that they radiate makes them truly lovely. This has been the attraction of many of the great saints. It should also be our attraction, dear friend. We should radiate the presence of God in our lives, not necessarily by our preaching, but by our loving.

We can hope for great things if we love God, great things in what we do for God and what God does for us. If we act from the love of Christ, the fruits of our activity will not be limited by our personal abilities. They will be the fruits of Christ's activity also, and no one can say what their limits will be. This is not pride, dear friend, but rather it is humble trust in God.

The virtue of hope, which is always connected to loving God, leads us to expect great things from God not only for others but for ourselves. "As it is written: 'No eye has seen, no ear has heard, no mind has conceived what God has prepared for those who love him'" (1 Cor. 2:9).

CHAPTER 83

• *Which Gives Us a Warning*

(See chapter 55 of *The Cloud*)

I do not think, dear friend, that we will ever, in this life, reach the point where we do not have to take care lest we fall into the sin of pride. This is the sin of the devil, and so it is one he delights to see in others. If we are not careful, it can frequently take the form of being judgmental toward others.

When the devil sees people who are obviously trying their best to pursue the loving search for God, he realizes that he will not be successful if he tempts them to something that is clearly evil. They will not be attracted to that. So he tries to ensnare them by something that might seem to them to be good. We might call this trap indiscreet zeal. It is a desire and an attempt to criticize others for being less holy or loving than we see ourselves to be.

People who fall into this temptation are always looking at others to find fault. They will use such expressions as, "Well, I may not be so perfect myself but . . . ," and then go on to condemn someone else. Or else they are always correcting others, nagging them or giving them advice. Of course, we must, at times, help others on the path to God. This is especially true if we are priests, teachers, or parents who have the care of souls. But even then we must remember that our own example is more powerful than any words we can say. A loving person is interested in the conversion of a sinner but not in chiding him or her. He is apt to err by kindness rather than severity. Is it not common sense (and loving sense) to realize that when our advice fails, there is no point in insisting on it by nagging or criticizing? It is time to try something else. Try loving!

CHAPTER 84
• *On How We Have a Well-Marked Path through Church Teachings and the Lives and Writings of the Saints*
(See chapter 57 of *The Cloud*)

Remember, dear friend, how Jesus told his disciples that he would not leave them orphans but would send the Holy Spirit to remind them of everything he taught them. "You know him (the Spirit of truth) for he lives with you and will be in you" (Jn. 14:17). Jesus is speaking here of the church. Through her teachings and through the examples and writings of the saints, we have ample instructions for the loving search. Look to the church then for your nourishment in the sacraments, especially the Eucharist. Look to the church for your instructions, especially in the Bible and the liturgical readings. There you will find what you need to run along the pathways of your loving search.

This little book, dear friend, expresses the traditional teachings of the church and reflects the practices of many of the great saints. It is based immediately, as you already know, on the ancient theological treatise called *The Cloud of Unknowing*. *The Cloud* itself is based on a sixth-century work by a monk called Dionysius. This, in turn, reflects the practice of the earliest Christians in their loving search for God. Only recently in a document issued from the Vatican, advising Christians on what they may receive from the traditions of the Eastern non-Christian religions, and what they must avoid, *The Cloud* was particularly recommended as authentically containing the Catholic tradition on contemplative prayer.

CHAPTER 85

• *On Different Devotions and How
They Relate to the Prayer of Loving*

Dear friend in God, out of the richness of her long and venerable tradition, the holy church offers us many and varied forms of devotions. Some of them are even said to come from Jesus himself, or his blessed mother, or one or other of the saints. They are given to us as aids to prayer. I am speaking here of such commendable devotions as the rosary, the stations of the cross, novenas, or special prayers to the virgin or saints. There is no need here for me to give you instructions on how to perform any of these devotions. Much has been written about them elsewhere. In themselves they are indeed holy practices and much to be recommended. When they proceed from a loving heart, they can indeed be expressions of the contemplative attitude. However, in the deepest form of contemplative prayers, without words or symbols, even these devotions give way to the will's silent embrace of God in darkness.

CHAPTER 86

• *A Warning against Superstition in our
Devotions*

I would warn you, dear friend, to avoid the tendency to associate questionable or even heretical and superstitious practices to these devotions. Let me explain what I mean. Recently in my travels I visited a church to spend some time in meditation before the blessed sacrament. Someone had recently distributed on the benches around the church some small leaflets with a prayer to St. Jude. Before the prayer there was printed in large letters, "This prayer has never been known to fail." I am afraid that this kind of thing verges on superstition.

One is given the "distinct impression" that this particular prayer with these specific words has a power that other prayers do not have. This, of course, is a great error. All prayers approved by the church have great power with God as do prayers said in your own words. I think it can be said that the power of any given prayer is directly based on the faith, love, and even the need of the one who prays.

Neither God nor the blessed mother nor the saints are particularly concerned with the wording of a prayer as long as it comes from a loving heart in faith and hope. Such prayers have never been known to fail! I must explain that last sentence more clearly. Prayer is not a method or power given to us so that we can order God around, or tell God how to run the world (or our own world). It is a way to express our love for God and our dependence on God's mercy. An essential part of every prayer, whether explicit or understood, must be: "if it is according to your will, O God!" This is how Jesus prayed (cf. Lk. 22:42).

We must also understand that in response to every authentic loving prayer (and even to prayers offered in desperation and some ignorance of God), God's response is greater than we can realize. God's answer to every prayer is Godself. We are constantly asking for lesser things when God wants to give us the greatest gift possible.

CHAPTER 87
· *How We Should Pray for the Greatest Gift*

I remember, as a child, one time I was praying for a new bicycle. Then I heard in a sermon that we did not ask enough from God, that God was willing to give us much more than we could conceive. Immediately I began to pray for two bicycles! Little did I realize that I was supposed to pray for *God*, and that in possessing God I would possess everything. It is not unlikely that I would have preferred a bicycle, but God understands the prayers of children and will take care of them. Yet even children must not be led to think that they can have every whim satisfied through prayer. Also they must be taught that God's will is to be preferred even when they pray for serious things, such as for a parent dying of cancer or for world peace.

CHAPTER 88

· What Is Meant When we Say that God Gives Godself in Answer to Prayer

The ultimate answer to every prayer, dear friend, is God's response: "Here I am." Our difficulty often is that we prefer something less than God (e.g., a bicycle! or a cancer cure!). God understands our weaknesses and our ignorance as well as our genuine needs. God's response is to be heard like this: "Here I am. I know your needs, your sufferings, your weaknesses. You have turned to me for help and I will not refuse you. Your way may be difficult, even as the way of the cross was difficult for Jesus, but I will take your hand and walk it with you. I want you to know this and to be comforted by it. You have my love and my strength to support you."

CHAPTER 89

· How Are We to Respond to Requests for Particular Devotions, Such as Were Made at Fatima

Now, dear friend, you may rightly ask me, if the form of our prayer makes no difference to God or the saints as long as it proceeds from love, how do you explain the specific devotions requested by our Lord or his blessed mother. I am thinking here of the nine first Fridays or the rosary devotions (coming from the Fatima visions and the Sacred Heart visions), and the promises made to those who perform them.

This is not difficult to understand. Our Lord or the blessed mother are simply using human ways to help us respond to our need for prayer. Particular suggestions, such as the nine first Fridays, give us something concrete to do and allow us to have an awareness that we are making a proper effort in our prayers. It is also a way to encourage us to persevere in our prayers, as Jesus told us in the parable about the unjust judge (Lk. 18:2f.).

We should not think that God prefers one devotion over another. We have many forms of devotion to suit many needs and many different kinds of people. We must avoid, dear friend, anything that smacks of superstition or oversimplistic literalness in our prayers. I think it remains to be said that the best form of personal prayer remains that prayer in which we seek union with God in love beyond words, beyond requests, and beyond thoughts. God will draw us to this prayer, either through our devotions, through instructions such as this book offers, or any other way God desires.

CHAPTER 90

• Which Tells How We Are Creatures both of Heaven and Earth

(See chapters 62 to 65 of *The Cloud*)

It is our glory and our tragedy, dear friend, to be creatures of both heaven and earth. We are made in the image and likeness of God, and so we share in heavenly realities. However, we are born into what the poets call "a bent world." Sociologists call it a society given over to selfish pursuits. Psychologists call it a series of defense mechanisms built to protect ourselves from the outside world. Theologians call it original sin. None of them are too sure exactly what it is or how it is transmitted, but all of them are quite positive of its reality and its harmful effects.

We are called by God's love, as made manifest in Jesus Christ, to restore God's image and likeness. As St. Paul tells us, "the first man (Adam) was of the dust of the earth, the second man (Jesus) from heaven. . . . And just as we have borne the likeness of the earthly man, so shall we bear the likeness of the man from heaven" (1 Cor. 15:47–49).

Our loving faculty, which we call the will, suffers along with our bodies from the effects of original sin. This is why the contemplative prayer of our loving search can sometimes be so difficult. "But thanks be to God; he gives us the victory through our Lord, Jesus Christ" (1 Cor. 15:57).

It is because we are creatures of earth that God became human. God turned the tables and took on *our* image and likeness so that we might be restored to *God's* image and likeness. And do you know, dear friend, what the common element is? Do you know what belongs to us, both earthly creatures and sharers of the divine? Here is the answer: "How great is the love the Father has lavished on us, that we should be called the children of God! And that is what we are!" (1 Jn. 3:1). Love is what restores in us the image of God.

CHAPTER 91

• *Our Likeness to God Is a Matter of Grace. It is a Gift Freely Given*

Each day, dear friend in God, when I celebrate the Eucharist, I pour a few drops of water into the chalice that holds the wine and say this prayer: "By the mingling of this water and wine, may we come to share in the divinity of Christ who humbled himself to share in our humanity." Think of it. Because we are in the image and likeness of God, because we do share in the heavenly realities, we are divinized. This is how the early church fathers described it. We become sharers in the very life of God. We enter into the very being of the Trinity, because we are in Christ, members of his body; we are brought back to the Father by the gracious power of the Holy Spirit.

This is not, dear friend in God, something we deserve or earn. It is given to us freely by God because God loves us. Do you see now why we must love each other? Our existence is meaningless without love. It is that in which we live and move and have our being. What we freely receive, we must freely give. In order for this love to be complete, we must share it. This is why Jesus tells us that love is the great commandment. This is why I say that there is really only one sin—to be unloving.

This oneness with God in love is a matter of faith, dear friend. However, our oneness with each other in love is a matter of everyday experience. "No one has ever seen God, but if we love one another, God lives in us and his love is made complete in us" (1 Jn. 2:5). We do not love others because they deserve it (although we know that they often do deserve it), but because we must love them. There is no other reaction we can have to other human beings except to love them, friend or foe, relative or stranger, benefactors or competitors.

Seek after love then and pursue it in the contemplative prayer of your loving search. Dip into this prayer as into a reservoir of living water; long for it as the deer longs for the running stream; wait for it and expect it as the watchman waits for the dawn. Receive it from the hands of your loving Father who pours it into your heart in the abundant overflowing of the Holy Spirit.

CHAPTER 92

• How God is Everywhere and We Need Go Nowhere to Possess God

(See chapter 68 of *The Cloud*)

This is the glory of loving God, dear friend: God is always available. Everything that is, is charged with God's presence. God fills every space, not as being contained, but as containing. In fact, it is impossible to escape God. God upholds all being by God's presence. God is, as the beautiful prayer of St. Patrick says, within us, without us, above us, below us, before us, behind us, on our right side and our left.

CHAPTER 93
· *How Certain Verses of Psalm 139 Are*
a Wonderful Expression of God's
Presence to Us

> Before a word is on my tongue
> You know it completely, O Lord.
> You hem me in—behind and before;
> You have laid your hand upon me.
> Such knowledge is too wonderful for me,
> Too lofty for me to attain.
> Where can I go from your Spirit?
> Where can I flee from your presence?
> If I go up to the heavens, you are there;
> If I make my bed in the depths, you are there.
> If I rise on the wings of the dawn,
> If I settle on the far side of the sea,
> Even there your hand will guide me,
> Your right hand will hold me fast.
> If I say, "Surely the darkness will hide me,
> And the light become night around me,"
> Even the darkness will not be dark to you;
> The night will shine like the day
> For darkness is as light to you.
>   (Ps. 139:4–12)

Truly, this is overwhelming, dear friend. Not only is God everywhere, but if we seek to flee from God, God is already present wherever we run to. God is even with us on the way. Is it not the sensible thing to surrender to God's love, to open ourselves to receive it fully in the prayer of our loving search?

We do not have to go anywhere to love God. God is here. God is waiting where we are. God will be friend, companion, father, mother, brother, sister, lover—whatever we need. Because God is all things to all men and women. Indeed such knowledge is too wonderful for us (vs. 6).

I think it will be obvious to you, dear friend, that God is not only present where we are and where we go, but God is present to us no matter *how* we are. Remember the beautiful marriage prayer where the husband and wife pledge to be present to each other "for better or for worse, for richer or for poorer, in sickness and in health, until death." This is because the union of husband and wife, a sacrament, must be a sign of the union of God and the individual soul (or with every soul—that is, the union of Christ and the church).

The beautiful Canticle of Canticles in the Bible is an expression of God's love in imagery taken from human courtship and married love. Such is our oneness with God that God cannot abandon us even if we wanted to abandon God. So we can and should seek union with God in our loving contemplative prayer wherever we are and in whatever condition, in sickness and health, joy and sorrow, good fortune and bad. We have the better part, the one thing necessary, and it will not be taken from us.

CHAPTER 94

• *How God Is Present Even When We Sin*

(See chapter 69 of *The Cloud*)

I have just said, dear friend, that we should seek loving, prayerful union with God wherever we are and in whatever condition. This means even if we have sinned and, indeed, especially if we have sinned. Even if we abandon God, God will not abandon us. The proof of this is in God's call for our love when we have sinned. God summons us back, again and again. God is truly a friend; God really loves us. If we try to get away from God, God will chase us down. God will not use force, but only loving persuasion, to bring about our return.

There is a lovely poem by Francis Thompson called, "The Hound of Heaven." He compares God to a hunting dog constantly following him as he seeks escape. He tries to hide from God in material goods, wealth, power, sex, and hatred. But no matter what he does, God pursues him and says, "All things betrayeth thee who betrayeth me." Finally he gives in to God's relentless following and surrenders in love to God.

Remember how I told you earlier about the elderly Poor Clare nun who said to me, "Father, everything leads to God . . . everything . . . everything!"

CHAPTER 95
• That Contemplative Prayer Is Not Limited to Extraordinary Experiences or to Extraordinary Saints
(See chapter 71 of *The Cloud*)

There has been, dear friend in God, in the recent past, an attitude that the contemplative prayer of our loving search was an extraordinary thing. It was thought to be limited to some few very holy people, probably contemplative monks and nuns. Certainly, the average Christian was not expected to be raised to such lofty heights. It was thought to be so different and so rare that it could be reached only with a great struggle. Then when it was given, it was thought to be some kind of mystic, ecstatic experience of spiritual delight.

No doubt there are such saints who have such experiences, but I am not concerned with them now. I am concerned, dear friend, with you and me. We too are called to love God and to delight in that love. The kind of contemplative meditation taught in this little book will help us to do this and to grow in that love.

It has never been my intention to teach, describe, or otherwise deal with extraordinary spiritual experiences. I will leave that to the theologians. I am simply speaking to children of God who seek to love their heavenly Father in the simple prayer of contemplative love. This prayer is neither different nor rare, as I am sure you realize by now. Do not listen to those who would tell you that contemplative prayer is above you or too difficult for you or reserved for people much holier than you.

As I have said, dear friend, I am concerned with the simple loving prayer of simple, loving people such as you and I. There are other approaches to contemplative prayer, perhaps even other ways to understand it. I do not criticize or disapprove of them. I simply do not teach them. If anyone is interested in other approaches, he or she is welcome to go to one of the many other authentic sources approved by the church.

CHAPTER 96

• *That Contemplation, like Other Forms of Prayer, Has Different Levels*
(See chapters 71 to 73 of *The Cloud*)

I think it is reasonable to say, dear friend in God, that there are different levels of contemplative prayer. However, I do not think that we should be overconcerned about them. God will lead each of us, in his or her own way, as God wills. Some theologians like to dwell on the different levels of loving prayer, make distinctions, formulate definitions, divisions, and the like. This is their business. No doubt some people will find it helpful to investigate their theories. I think, however, that Thomas Merton, no mean theologian himself, was right when he said that when more attention was given to the theories about contemplation than to its practice, it was a sure sign of spiritual decline.

So let us rejoice with all who delight in loving God, no matter what approach they use or how advanced they are. We are one with them in that very love we all share and experience in the prayer of our loving search for God.

CHAPTER 97
· *Which Offers Advice to Discover*
if This was Written for You
(See chapter 74 of *The Cloud*)

Dear friend, does this little book appeal to you? Do you resonate
to its descriptions of love, both God's and your own? Does it seem
to be reasonable in its demands and promises? Do you find it possible to follow both in its instructions and in its application? If you
can answer in the affirmative to these questions, then this little
book is definitely for you.

Let me beg you, at this point, to follow two more instructions.
I have covered many areas of the loving search in this little book,
and have given you a great deal of matter to digest and to remember.
I think it would be worth your while to read it a second and even
a third time. You will find that several readings will clarify things
for you, and will also bring out important teachings that you may
not have previously noticed. This is only to be expected in a book
that tries to deal so practically with your loving search for God.

The short chapters and the titles of the chapters are designed to
make reading easier. Also, the table of contents in the front of the
book will make it easier to find special sections you may want to
look up again.

If you find this book helpful, dear friend, I will be very pleased.
What a joy it is to know that we are united in the heart of God
and that we will continue to meet in God's love. If you know of
others who are in the same loving search or would like to be, please
share this book with them.

CHAPTER 98
· *Which Contains a Final Statement
about the Call to Contemplation and
Finishes the Section of this Little Book
Based on* The Cloud of Unknowing
(See chapter 75 of *The Cloud*)

Let me review for you, dear friend, what I would consider the
qualifications for anyone to effectively seek the contemplative love
for God as described in this little book. First, and most obvious,
is the desire and the determination to live a good Christian life. By
no means does it mean that you must be perfect. If that were the
case, then no one could pursue the loving search. You must be
willing to make use of the normal available means the church offers
for the Christian life. This includes, of course, as we have said
previously, the sacraments, the Mass, the pursuit of the virtues and
the corporal and spiritual works of mercy. All of these are expected
from any decent Christian.

There is something further that you must recognize if you are
to consider that you are called to the contemplative meditation of
this loving search for God. You must feel an interior attraction to
the simple prayer described in this little book. It does not have
to take the place of all your usual devotions, but you should have
a desire to give yourself, now and then, with greater or lesser frequency, to this work of loving God. If God is calling you, you
will certainly feel this desire. It is a great blessing, indeed, and you
should be very grateful for it.

If you should begin this loving prayer and then find that you are
neglecting it, you should not despair or give it up altogether. The
desire to love God increases as we give ourselves to that love in
prayer. Sometimes we may not even feel the desire, but we still
know somehow that this prayer is for us. This will be true even
without consolation or comfort.

Look for and respond to that gentle tug of love, that tiny stirring
in your heart that is the sure sign of God's calling. Do not be

concerned with your unworthiness. You are unworthy. If you were ever to feel that you were worthy, then you would be in real trouble! Do not be concerned with what you are, or what you have been. God is more interested in what you desire to be and in what God wishes you to become.

I wish you great joy in your love for God, dear friend. Give yourself freely to God's love and you will bound forward in the loving search in great strides. Do not look back, only forward. May God give to you and to all who love God peace, wisdom, and joy.

CHAPTER 99

• Which Begins a Consideration of How Loving God Must Involve Loving Oneself and One's Neighbor

You will recall, dear friend in God, that when Jesus was asked what was the greatest commandment, he said in reply two things. First, he said, love God, and second, love your neighbor as yourself for the love of God. In fact there are three things involved here: 1) love of God; 2) love of self; 3) love of neighbor. These three are so interrelated that any one or two of them is impossible without the other(s).

So far in this little book, I have been teaching about love of God—that is, God's love for us and our love for God. Now I would like to say something about the other two great loves; neighbor and self. Notice, first of all, that Jesus says we must love our neighbor as ourself *for the love of God*. Thus love of God is the motivation for the other two loves. It is impossible to love God without loving neighbor and self, and it is impossible to love neighbor and self without loving God. As St. John tells us, "If you do not love your brother whom you can see, how can you love God whom you do not see" (1 John). The spiritual masters have always insisted that the only authentic measure of our love for God is found in our love for one another.

Thomas Merton, himself a hermit, says that a hermit who withdraws from the world, and even from his monastic family, must do so for the sake of the world and his monastic brothers. A hermit seeks solitude to draw closer to God that he may, in the mystery of the body of Christ, somehow draw the whole world with him.

CHAPTER 100

· While the Motive for Loving Neighbor Is the Love of God, the Norm Is Love of Self

As long as our love for one another, dear friend, is motivated by love of God, it will remain secure. Sometimes we do not see in our neighbors those things that would prompt us to love them. That is why we must turn to God for our motivation. Remember how Jesus on the cross forgave his tormentors. Surely they had not endeared themselves to him by their actions, but his love for God was so great he could not help but love even his enemies.

But how much should we love our neighbor and what should be the norm for that love? Jesus made this very clear when he said to love our neighbor *as we love ourselves.* Love for self is basic to our very being. It is built in, as it were. In fact, it dominates our life and has a crucial part to play in our every thought, word, and activity. This is not necessarily selfishness although selfishness is the negative side of self-love. We must love ourselves or we cannot love our neighbor or even God. See how the three loves are one: love your neighbor as yourself for the love of God!

Of course it follows, dear friend, that if we love others as we love ourselves, it is impossible for our self-love to be selfish. We can then freely use our love for self as the norm and measure of our love for others. This is, of course, what is meant by the golden rule: Do unto others whatever you would have them do unto you.

CHAPTER 101
• Is Self-Love Easy or to Be Taken for Granted?

I do not think, dear friend, that self-love can be taken for granted. Indeed, it is not always easy. I think that people who engage in "worm theology," as I have previously explained it, have difficulty in self-love. They are the ones with a low self-esteem who have been led to believe that they are worthless, no good, and without redeeming qualities. This was done early in their childhood by some significant adult and they have come to accept it without question.

O my friend, if only we could be led to take God, our Father, as the significant adult in our lives. Then we would know that we are loved. It is precisely because God loves us that we are worth loving. God does not create junk! God creates beloved children in whom God finds pleasure and joy. God proved that love beyond question by assuming our humanity in Jesus and dying for us—for greater love has no one than that he or she lay down his or her life for a friend. We must not only love our neighbor for the love of God, but we must love ourselves also.

I saw once two little pictures that said very appealingly what I am trying to convey in this chapter. The first picture shows a little girl about five years old sitting dejectedly on the stairs in front of her home. She has just been reprimanded for being naughty and says to herself, "I am going to go and eat worms" (worm theology!). In the second picture, however, she brightens up, changes her mind, and says with a smile, "I don't care; Jesus loves me!"

CHAPTER 102
• *How We Can Find Our True Value in Jesus*

Dear friend in God, if ever you should find yourself engaging in any form of self-hatred or low self-esteem, throw yourself on Christ. Surely you cannot question that the Father loves Jesus, the Son, in whom God is well pleased. Surely you cannot question that Jesus loves you when he gave his life for your sake. He has told us that he loves us even as the Father loves him. He identifies with us, calls us to be his friends, and invites us to be one with him even as he is one with the Father. He gives us his Holy Spirit, the Spirit of love to bind us to him with such a oneness that we become ourselves the body of Christ.

CHAPTER 103
• *In Which We See Our Self-Worth in Terms of God's Affirmation of Love*

God's word in the scriptures, dear friend, is a word of power. It goes forth from God and it will not return to God in vain. I would like to share with you some of God's powerful words proving this love.

I have gone through the entire Bible to see every inspired reference to God's love for us. I have chosen only a fraction of them for your encouragement. Read them. Reflect on them. Receive them and believe in them. They are for you. Rejoice in what they tell you. Take them to heart and cherish them.

And God passed in front of Moses proclaiming,
"The Lord, the Lord, the compassionate and gracious God,
Slow to anger, abounding in love and faithfulness"
(Ex. 34:6).

Know therefore that the Lord your God is God;
He is the faithful God, keeping his covenant of love
(Dt. 7:9).

Give thanks to the Lord for he is good;
His love endures forever (1 Chron. 16:34).

Turn, O Lord, and deliver me;
Save me because of your unfailing love (Ps. 6:4).

Your love, O Lord, reaches to the heavens,
Your faithfulness to the skies (Ps. 36:5).

How priceless is your unfailing love!
Both high and low among men find refuge in the shadow of
your wings (Ps. 36:7).

Because your love is better than life,
My lips will glorify you (Ps. 63:3).

I love those who love me and those who seek me find me
(Pro. 8:17).

Though the mountains be shaken
And the hills be removed,
Yet my unfailing love for you
Will not be shaken nor my covenant of
Peace be removed, says the Lord (Is. 54:10).

The Lord appeared to us in the past saying:
I have loved you with an everlasting love.
I have drawn you with loving kindness (Jer. 31, 3).

I will betroth you to me forever. . . .
In righteousness and justice,
In love and compassion (Hos. 2:19).

The Lord your God is with you,
He is mighty to save,

THE LOVING SEARCH FOR GOD · 103

He will take great delight in you;
He will quiet you with his love (Zeph. 3:17).

• Which Continues the Proofs of God's Love

As I have loved you so you must love one another
(Jn. 13:34).

He who loves me will be loved by my Father
And I too will love him (Jn. 14:21).

As the Father has loved me,
So have I loved you.
Remain in my love (Jn. 15:9).

Father, I have made you known to them
And will continue to make you known
In order that the love you have for me
May be in them and that I myself may be in them
(Jn. 17:26).

Hope does not disappoint us
Because God has proved out his love.
Into our hearts by the Holy Spirit
Whom he has given us (Rom. 5:5).

God demonstrates his own love for us in this:
While we were still sinners, Christ died for us (Rom. 5:8).

In love God predestined us to be adopted as his sons
(Eph. 1:5).

Because of his great love for us,
God, who is rich in mercy, made us all alive with Christ
even when we were dead in transgressions (Eph. 2:4).

I pray that you, being rooted and established in love,
May have power, together with all the saints,
To grasp how wide and long and high and deep is the love
of Christ
And to know this love that surpasses knowledge,
That you may be filled to the measure of all the fullness of
God (Eph. 3:17).

Be imitators of God, therefore, as dearly loved children
And live a life of love
Just as Christ loved us and gave himself up for us
(Eph. 5:2).

When the kindness and love of God our Savior appeared
He saved us, not because of righteous things we had done,
But because of his mercy (Tit. 3:5).

How great is the love the Father has lavished on us,
That we should be called children of God (1 Jn. 3:1).

This is how we know what love is;
Jesus Christ laid down his life for us (1 Jn. 3:16).

Let us love one another
For love comes from God (1 Jn. 4:7).

God is love (1 Jn. 4:8).

This is love, not that we love God,
But that he loved us and sent his son (1 Jn. 4:10).

Since God so loved us, dear friends,
We also ought to love one another (1 Jn. 4:11).

No one has ever seen God;
But if we love one another, God lives in us
And his love is made complete in us (1 Jn. 4:12).

And so we know and rely on the love God has for us.

God is love. Whoever lives in love lives in God,
And God in him (1 Jn. 4:16).

We love because God first loved us (1 Jn. 4:19).

Keep yourself in God's love
As you wait for the mercy of our Lord Jesus Christ
To bring you to eternal life (Jude 1:21).

CHAPTER 105
· *Which Tells a Story Illustrating the*
Transforming Power of Loving and of
God's Love

I would like to share with you, dear friend in God, a story that
helps to illustrate how God views a true lover. This story is inspired
by a chapter in C. S. Lewis's *The Great Divorce*. It is adapted here
for my own purposes.

A man is given the extraordinary opportunity to take a tour of
heaven, guided by one of the great archangels who stands before
the most high God. He sees many wonderful sights. Perhaps the
most wonderful of all occurs when he walks with the archangel
down a beautiful mountain path leading into a lovely valley. With
the clarity of vision possible only in heaven he sees, on the mountainside opposite him, on the other side of the valley, a magnificent vision.

Slowly wending its way toward the valley, there is a huge procession of rejoicing beings. At the head of the procession he sees many
cherubim, seraphim, and numerous varieties of angels singing and
dancing, doing cartwheels in the air and filling the valley with their
glorious chorus. To his amazement he sees that these are followed
by none other than Adam and Eve, who in turn are followed by
the rejoicing patriarchs, Abraham and Sarah, Isaac, Jacob and their
spouses, Joseph and all his brothers.

Then, singing and dancing with lutes, harps, and drums, come
the great prophets of the Old Testament. Then close at hand are

the four evangelists, Matthew, Mark, Luke, and John. The solemn Paul of Tarsus is there dancing hand in hand with St. Stephen. Then follows 144 martyrs of the early church, the great doctors and fathers, Jerome, Basil, Augustine, and Gregory the Great. Also present and joining in the glorious chorus are the saints of the middle ages, Bernard, Bruno, Francis, Clare, and Dominic, followed by more recent holy men and women such as Teresa of Avila, John of the Cross, Ignatius of Loyola, Maria Goretti, and Thérèse of Lisieux. Then a mighty archangel walks grandly down speaking with a voice that shatters the oak trees: "My ways are not your ways, says the Lord. As far as the heavens are from the earth, so far are my ways from your ways."

Our traveler stands still in astonishment at this marvelous spectacle. Finally he sees the reason for it all. Coming down the mountainside at the very end are four of the greatest angels of the heavenly host carrying on their shoulders a golden chair wherein is seated a woman of great beauty.

He turns to his angelic guide. Thinking that surely this woman must be the blessed mother of God, he barely manages to gasp out his question. "Is that . . . is that . . . ?" He cannot even finish. The archangel laughs and replies, "No, no, that's Molly Schultz! You wouldn't know her. She lived in your city in shantytown. She was a scrubwoman but she loved much. She is one of the Great Ones here."

CHAPTER 106

• Which Continues Exhortations to True Love of Self

Do you see now, dear friend in God, why you are lovable. God makes you so. It does not really depend on what you have done or have neglected to do. In spite of your past, your sins, your selfishness, in spite of what anybody else may have told you, God does love you and calls you to love God, to love yourself and to love others.

CHAPTER 107
• How the Way in which God Loves Us Should Determine the Way We Love Ourselves and Others. Unconditional Love

We can also see, dear friend, that God's love for us is unconditional. This means that God loves us without conditions. We did not have to do anything to earn God's love and we may even do things that should (according to our way of thinking) lose God's love. We see this especially in the fact that we are told God loved us when we were still in our sins. "This is love, not that we love God but that he loved us and sent his Son as an atoning sacrifice for our sins" (1 Jn. 4:10).

God does not bargain with us. In spite of some Old Testament passages to the contrary, we see in the love of Christ, a total commitment of love for us without conditions. God loves us because God is love. God does not say, "Do this and I will love you, or do not do that and I will love you." He says, "You are my children and I love you. I love you for better or for worse, in sickness and in health, in sin and in grace. I love you without conditions, without qualifications. I will continue to love you no matter what you do. I will love you even if you forget me, repudiate me, or reject me. I will call you back to me by my love. My door is never closed to you. I love you so much that I will even allow you to turn your back on me if that is what you want. Even then I will not cease to offer you my love." This, dear friend, is unconditional love—the love of God.

CHAPTER 108

• *How God's Love Is a Model*

"Dear friend, let us love one another, for love comes from God; everyone who loves has been born of God and knows God . . . since God so loved us, we also ought to love one another" (1 Jn. ch. 4). Do you know what this means, dear friend in God? It means that we have to love ourselves and one another with the same unconditional love that comes from God.

In particular I would like to stress here that we must love ourselves unconditionally. This obviously is not selfishness. It is not a license to sin or to harm ourselves in any way. It is rather a call to self-perfection, to fulfillment, to develop to its fullness the love that God has poured into our hearts, so that we may more and more resemble the beloved Son who has re-created us by the Holy Spirit in God's loving image.

This also means that we may never cease to love ourselves no matter what we do or may have done. You see, dear friend, it is only by loving ourselves unconditionally that we can safeguard our love for others. They must be loved *as we love ourselves.* And because we love both ourselves and others for the love of God, it must be without conditions.

Do you realize how freeing this is? Our love plans no limitations or expectations on others. We are grateful for what we receive from them but we love them no matter what. We make no demands. We do not suffer setbacks when our expectations are not met. Our love is without conditions. We do not seek revenge; we do not suffer the pangs of jealousy. We forgive our enemies and seek to do good to those who hate us. Our love is unconditional!

CHAPTER 109

• Which Asks How Realistic Unconditional Love Is and Suggests How to Achieve It

At this point, dear friend, it would not surprise me to hear you object, "Unconditional love is truly divine. In fact it is so divine, that it seems impossible for a mere human being like myself to practice it at all." This is a reasonable statement but one that forgets that love comes from God. We do not love with a mere human love but with God's love. We have the example of Jesus and are empowered by the Holy Spirit.

Remember that love is patient. We cannot expect this kind of perfection from the beginning, but we must make a start. "Love always trusts, always hopes, always perseveres" (1 Cor. 13:7). We know, dear friend, that we have made a great start in our loving search when we are united to God's love in contemplative meditation. By trusting in this loving prayer, we will gradually see God's unconditional love manifesting itself in our lives, as we learn more and more how truly to love ourselves and others.

CHAPTER 110

• Using the Memory, Imagination, and Intellect as Well as the Emotions as Aids to Loving

I have been teaching you, dear friend in God, an approach to loving God which goes beyond words and images to immediate loving union. I have taught you how to "escape the snares of the senses and the mazes of the mind" to come to the Word unspoken, that is recited in the darkness at the very center of your being. I have also said that our Memory, Imagination, Intellect, and Emotions have their proper place in our prayer lives even if not in the particular kind of contemplation that is so much a part of our loving search for God. I would now like to teach you a method of using all these faculties as an aid to loving your neighbor.

CHAPTER 111
· Which Teaches a Way of Loving Called Compassion Meditation

I am sure you realize, dear friend, that when we love somebody as God wants us to love, it must be a complete, unconditional love reaching into all levels of our existence. It must involve not only our intellects but even our emotions.

This is not easy, especially when we have a good reason to be ill-disposed to someone—for example, when someone has hurt us. We may reach the point, through God's grace, where we can say that we have forgiven them, but still have emotions in our hearts that are not in accord with that forgiveness. We have forgiven but do not feel that we have done so. The compassion meditation will help us to forgive on every level, even the emotional.

CHAPTER 112
· How Love of Neighbor Is Not an Abstract or Disembodied Reality

Dear friend in God, even God, to show the divine love for us, chose not to remain disembodied. God took flesh in our Savior Jesus Christ so that we could relate to him and see a human demonstration of God's love. We have been speaking in this little book of union with God in the loving search through contemplative prayer. We have also insisted, in the most authentic Catholic tradition, that the love of God so experienced and so enhanced would inevitably find expression also in love of self and one another. We are marvelously disposed to love one another through our experience, even in the darkness of contemplative prayer, of our love for God.

Because we share in the human, earthly realities as well as the heavenly ones, even as Jesus did, our love can be facilitated by our human understanding of ourselves and of others. I would now like to share with you some ideas that may contribute to that mutual understanding.

The glory of the human race is that we all reflect the image of God in different ways. Indeed, no two of us are alike. Thus we are able to mirror in almost unlimited ways the love of God as we live out that love in our daily lives. We must understand, dear friend, that the living out of this love expresses itself not only in those closest to us but extends beyond them. You have heard it said that charity begins at home. This means that if you are to love others at all, it must begin with those closest to you. Once begun, love then must overflow even to those who are far away (that is, alienated) from you. I would like to teach the compassion meditation, which seeks to concretize your love, beginning "at home" and then extending beyond your immediate circle.

CHAPTER 113

• Which Introduces the First Step of the Compassion Meditation

Dear friend in God, if you wish to experience this compassion meditation, just go along with me and follow my instructions step by step. You are going to select three persons whom you relate to on three different levels. The first person will be someone whom you love. You may select anyone for whom you feel an emotional love. This may be a person from any period of your life. It must be someone whom you presently love and for whom you wish every possible good and every possible blessing from God. It could be your father, or mother, a child, or any other relative or simply a friend.

Using your memory and imagination, summon this beloved person before you. Let me stress here that you are dealing with a real person with whom you have a real, emotional relationship. This compassion meditation will probably increase that loving relationship. This will be true even if your beloved is dead. In God there is no death. The church teaches that we still have communion with the dead who are with God. For this meditation we want to experience that communion even emotionally.

Recall your beloved as vividly as you can. Let him or her be present to you in their most lovable fashion. Recapture that love so that you feel it in your heart as well as you know it in your mind. Dwell on it, relish it, even feel it grow. Think of the reasons for that love, how it is reciprocated, how it began, how it increased, how it still abides with you. Appreciate your beloved as a gift from God, a reflection of God's love for you. Now, in your own words, offer a prayer to God in thanksgiving for your beloved and for what he or she means to you. Let this prayer be brief or lengthy as you feel inclined.

Now in a spirit of faith and love, before God, speak to your beloved. Tell him or her that you love him or her. Tell him or her how much and why. Tell him or her how grateful you are that he or she came into your life and is still a significant part of it. Remember, dear friend, this is true even if your beloved is dead! There is no death for those who have received life from Jesus Christ.

If there is anything to be said that you feel should be said to your beloved, say it now. Perhaps there is some unfinished business between you, maybe an apology, or a declaration of gratitude that you feel has not been adequately given yet. Let this be brief and simple or detailed and lengthy. If it is of any help to you, you can even write it down in the form of a letter, but do it in the presence of your beloved as your love makes him or her present.

Now speak directly to your beloved with the certain knowledge that what you are saying will also be a prayer before God. You may use your own words or use the ones I offer you here.

CHAPTER 114
· *Which Contains the Words That You*
Will Speak to Your Beloved and Offer to
Him or Her as a Prayer before Your
Loving God

The following words, dear friend in God, are my own poor
effort to suggest to you what you might say to your beloved whom
you have summoned to your presence in this compassion meditation. Be free to use them as they are given here, to change them,
add to or subtract from them, as you feel inclined. Address your
beloved prayerfully and lovingly in this way:

You are my friend and I love you.
Your love is a blessing to me and I thank God for you.
I wish for you from God every possible blessing.
May you be happy.
May you be free.
May you be loving.
May you be loved.
May you know every blessing that God wills for you.
May you experience the fullness of the Holy Spirit.
May you be enriched by the prayers and examples of the
    saints and angels.
May you and I constantly grow closer in God's holy love.
May God bring you to the fullest completion of your
    talents, abilities, and aspirations.
May joy and peace proceed from your heart and surround
    you always.
May everyone love you and wish you well.
May God's loving care protect you.
May God's guidance lead you forward.
May all your actions proceed from God and find their
    completion in God.
May you love even as you are loved.

You are my friend and I love you.
Just be present now to your beloved for a few moments in
silence, feeling your love.

CHAPTER 115

• *The Second Step in the Compassion*
Meditation, a Neutral Person

And now, dear friend, you are going to pick someone else whom
I refer to as a neutral person. This should be someone whom you
do not really know. It could be a mere acquaintance or someone
you have never met at all. The only requirement is that it be a real
person whom you have contacted somehow directly or indirectly. It
could even be someone you saw on television or in the newspaper, a
grocery clerk, a taxi driver, or the person who sat next to you on
a bus or in church.

Using your imagination, summon this neutral person before you
as concretely and vividly as possible. Now turn to the first person,
your beloved, and ask him or her for permission to share your
mutual love with this indifferent or neutral person. Speak to him
or her and offer the same prayer you offered before to your beloved. Offer the same sentiments, the same emotional feeling, and
the same unconditional love. You will be amazed at how you will
be able to do this. Love shared is not love diminished but love
increased.

CHAPTER 116

• In which We Choose a Third Person for our Compassion Meditation, an Enemy

And now, dear friend, we will choose a third person for our compassion meditation. This will be an enemy. Perhaps you will say, "But I do not have any enemies!" This may indeed be so. You could be truly blessed in this way. However, I have discovered that people who say this, after a bit of reflection, will often change their minds.

Allow me to explain what we mean by an enemy by asking some questions. Is there anyone in your life, past or present, living or dead, whom you have not forgiven—even emotionally. This consideration should reach back even to your earliest childhood. Is there anyone toward whom you feel anger, resentment, or jealousy? Is there someone whom you may feel you have forgiven but whom you sometimes think about with a certain amount of emotional irritation or even anger? Is there any figure in your life, past or present, or even any historical figure whom you resent or for whom you do not feel compassion? Remember that God loves every one of these people. God loves them unconditionally and this is the way you are expected to love them. "Love your neighbor as yourself for the love of God."

Please remember, dear friend, that when Jesus was asked whom we were to regard as our neighbor, he told the parable of the good Samaritan. The Jews of Jesus' time hated the Samaritans and this hatred was reciprocated. It was the result of centuries of religious, political, and emotional conflict. It was a great shock to Jesus' listeners to hear that Samaritans, their traditional enemies, were to be regarded as neighbors and were to be loved. It is also to be noted that the Jew who fell among robbers and whom the good Samaritan cared for was not a "personal" enemy of that particular Samaritan—they simply did not know each other, but both had inherited the traditional enmity belonging to their ethnic groups.

Can you see now, dear friend, how we must extend the notion of enemy even as we must extend the notion of neighbor? It has been my personal experience, unfortunately, that the longer I reflect on this matter, the more I find, in my own life, feelings of prejudice and resentment. These may be directed toward acquaintances or groups (such as foreign governments and armies, drug dealers, murderers or politicians, or even churchmen). It could even include persons or groups I know about only through my readings in history!

CHAPTER 117

• *In which We Seek to Make Our Enemies Our Friends*

Was it not Abraham Lincoln who said the best way to get rid of enemies was to make them friends? In point of fact, this is what Jesus said also. If you love your enemy, he or she is no longer an enemy, at least from your point of view. We must remember that God loved us when we were enemies. When we were in sin, God loved us. This is the only way we could have been freed from our sin.

It is also good for us to recall here, dear friend in God, that when we harbor anger, resentment, or hatred toward someone else, we are the losers. Usually such feelings have little or no actual effect on our enemy, but they do us personally great harm. Thus when we love our enemies, we ourselves receive the primary benefits, even if that is not our primary intention.

CHAPTER 118
• Which Concludes the Compassion Meditation

At this point in our compassion meditation, we have three persons before us: the beloved, the once neutral person, and the enemy. Now, dear friend, turn to your first two persons and ask their permission to share their love, even emotionally, with your enemy. Feel this love, recapture its sentiments, and turn to your enemy and offer before him or her the very same prayer (found in chapter 114) you offered before the others.

You may not find this very easy to do, but with God's grace you will find it possible. You may even find it helpful or necessary to repeat this compassion meditation, using the same enemy, several times, before you feel that your forgiveness and compassion is sufficiently deep. It even may have to be repeated again over a period of time if you sense your resentment reasserting itself. Rejoice, dear friend, in your efforts to love. Nothing can be more pleasing to God or more beneficial to yourself and to the world.

CHAPTER 119
• Which Begins a Consideration on the Lord's Prayer

The loving search for God, dear friend, is greatly facilitated by the Lord's Prayer. You may be surprised to hear it but when Jesus gave the Our Father to his disciples, he was not really giving them a prayer to memorize. Please understand me correctly. We have all memorized the Our Father and we say it many times. We should do so. However, it still remains true that when Jesus answered the request of his disciples, "Lord teach us how to pray," he did not do this by giving them a specific prayer to memorize and recite word for word.

We know this quite clearly from the context. The disciples did not ask for a prayer. They asked to be taught *how* to pray. John the Baptist taught his disciples how to pray, they reminded Jesus. Then they requested that Jesus too perform this task, which they saw as normal for a rabbi; "Teach us how to pray." We see this incident reported three times in three different gospels. In each account there is a different rendition of the Lord's Prayer. The one we commonly say is the one found in St. Matthew's Gospel but the prayer as seen in St. Luke and in St. Mark differs. This alone should tell us that the gospel accounts are not interested in giving us a specific prayer to recite word for word.

Then what did Jesus intend that we do? This is easy enough to answer. Jesus was simply answering the request that he teach his disciples how to pray. You see, dear friend in God, Jesus was teaching a *method* of prayer.

CHAPTER 120

• *Which Considers the Our Father as a Method of Prayer Rather Than a Prayer to Be Recited*

It should be very helpful to us, dear friend in God, to learn from Jesus *how* to pray. By the words of the Our Father, Jesus is giving us a series of dispositions, an attitude from which our prayers should proceed. Whenever we pray, with whatever words and for whatever purpose, our prayer should proceed from the background, the convictions, and the desires that are expressed in the Lord's Prayer. Jesus gives us even a priority for our prayers by listing in order of importance the dispositions we should have.

To understand the Lord's Prayer in this way—that is, as a series of dispositions that motivate our prayers—it is necessary to meditate on this prayer. We must consider seriously the meanings found in each phrase. When I first began the practice of "thinking" or "discoursive" meditation, as distinct from contemplative meditation, I used to meditate frequently on the Lord's Prayer. At first in a twenty-minute period I would go through the entire prayer, considering briefly the meaning of each phrase. Then I noticed that in a twenty-minute period I would not be able to get through the entire prayer, because I would want to dwell longer on some particular phrase. Eventually I found that I would find myself spending the entire meditation period on just the first two words or even on the first word, "Our."

CHAPTER 121
· *A Consideration of the First Disposition Jesus Teaches Us in the Our Father*

The first disposition Jesus teaches us, dear friend in God, is that when we pray, we must be aware always that we are praying to a father. We are taught this because it is a truth we must acknowledge, and also because it is a truth intended to give us great encouragement. We have a personal, intimate, loving relationship with the God to whom we pray. Thus, Jesus wants us to understand that we should pray with confidence, with great hope, faith, and love.

There is another very important thing Jesus desires that we realize when we pray to a father. He wants us to know that we are children of God, made to God's image and likeness, and that we should seek only those things in prayer that will enhance that image. Thus our first desire should be for a growth in love, in faith, and in hope. These are precisely the things that bring us closer to our God image, the ways in which we are graced to resemble our Father.

Jesus also wants us to realize that this is a two-way street. If we pray to God as to a father, God responds to us as to sons and daughters. God showers us with blessings proceeding from paternal love and fatherly wisdom. Jesus wants us to look at the relationship we see existing between ideal, earthly fathers and their children, and to extend that loving relationship to God.

CHAPTER 122

· *What It Means to Pray to a Father*

So, dear friend, Jesus wants us to pray to a father. This is the first attitude or disposition that should be present—in any prayer that we offer. How encouraging this is! When we are in need, we can go to a father. When we want consolation, we can go to a father. When we want love, we can go to a father. When we want strength, hope, we can go to a father. When we feel like failures, when we are weak, ill, sinful, tired, hungry, we can go to a father.

Do not ask for less than this. Do not seek something less than the response of a loving father. Do you know what that response will be? It will be Godself. God will say to us: "My beloved child, I hear you. You are precious to me and I will give you everything that I have. Even though you are asking me for something less, I will give you myself! I will be with you. I will hold your hand and accompany you through your trials. I will never abandon you. Your present journey, no matter how hard it seems, is leading you to me and I will be with you every step of the way." How great is the love the Father has lavished upon us that we should be called children of God (1 Jn. 3:1).

CHAPTER 123

· *How Much Is Contained in That Little Word* Our. *How We Are One with Jesus*

Dear friend, I have been stressing the connection between our love for God, for ourselves, and one another. Jesus, of course, does this also. Remember how he said, "As the Father has loved me, so have I loved you. Remain in my love" (Jn. 15, 9). This then is the first disposition we should have when we pray, not merely to *a* father, but to *our* father. Jesus wants us to be aware that we are one with him, his brothers and sisters, and that it is to his father and our father that we pray. "If you knew me, you would know my Father also" (Jn. 8:20). "On that day you will realize that I am in my Father, and you are in me and I am in you" (Jn. 14:20).

Our attitude then, in whatever prayer we offer, is that we are praying together with Jesus to his father and our father. What a joy this is and what consolation it should give us!

CHAPTER 124
· *Which Greatly Expands Our Understanding of the Phrase* Our Father

We cannot, dear friend in God, stop here. The word *our* not only unites us to Jesus, but expresses our union with one another in Jesus. When we pray to our Father, we pray together with every man, woman, and child on the face of the earth, below the earth, and above the earth, past, present, and future. We are all brothers and sisters of a common father and Jesus insists that when we pray, we must pray with an awareness of this. "When you pay, say, Our Father!"

Do you realize what this means? Do you understand that according to the method of prayer Jesus teaches us, we must have the attitude that we pray in acknowledgment that we are all God's children. This means that we may never exclude anyone from our prayer. When we say "our Father" we put our arms around the shoulders of everyone of God's children—barring none! Now do you see why our love must be all-embracing, why we must love even our enemies, why no one can be excluded?

Have you ever heard the prayer of the old Yankee farmer? "God bless me and my wife, my son, John, and his wife. Us four—No More!" This is not a prayer at all. This man is not praying to *our* father. He is not praying as Jesus taught.

CHAPTER 125

• *How We Can Use Just the First Two*
Words of the Lord's Prayer

Can you see now, dear friend, that Jesus teaches us that the first
consideration we must have when we pray is that we are praying
together with him to his father and also that we are praying together
with all humankind to our father. It would be very good for us if
we could concretize this first attitude into our daily lives. I would
like to suggest a practical way to do this.

Take as your prayer for one day (at least as a start) the two words
"Our Father." Be aware that whenever you say them you are going
toward the Father with one arm about Jesus' shoulder and the other
about the shoulders of all your brothers and sisters. Resolve today
that you are going to say that simple two-word prayer at least fifty
times. When you see someone, anyone, at home, outside, on the
television set, in the newspaper, celebrating, rejoicing, succeeding
in some task, or whatever, embrace that person together with Jesus
and pray, "Our Father."

If you are angry, or puzzled, or hurt by someone, do the same.
Then you will begin to see what Jesus meant by a method of prayer
that begins with "Our Father."

CHAPTER 126

• *How the Attitude Jesus Teaches Us*
Must Extend beyond the Mere Words of
the Prayer

There is something very important, dear friend, that we must be
reminded of here. Jesus was very explicit about this when he said,
"Not everyone who says to me, Lord, Lord, will enter the kingdom of heaven, but only he who does the will of my Father" (Mt.
7:21). He is telling us that our prayer must extend over into our

actions. It is not enough to acknowledge that we are all children of the Father in heaven; we must act upon it. The joys and the successes, as well as the sorrows and needs, of all men and women, are our joys, our sorrows. They are the successes and the needs of our brothers and sisters.

But what can we do, you might ask? How can we respond to the needs and celebrate the joys of the entire world? This is indeed a reasonable question and one that I constantly have to ask myself. Here in Israel where I am writing this little book, I have many friends and people who come to me for spiritual counseling who have stories that would break the coldest heart. They are, for the most part, Palestinians who have suffered grievously under the occupation by the Israeli Defense Forces (army). Almost all of them have or have had family members arrested, often for years, without recourse to civil rights. Frequently they are tortured, a procedure defended by the High Court of this supposedly civilized country. For the slightest provocation, or for none at all, their identity cards are torn up. This leaves them as people with no legal existence. They cannot work, travel, or receive aid. If stopped by the military, they will be arrested (for not having the very cards the military confiscated!). Recently several families I know (each with five to ten children) had their homes bulldozed as punishment because their teenage sons threw stones at military vehicles. Some of the children have had their arms broken by the soldiers. At times some of these people have spoken to me with tears in their eyes, wanting to know why the United States supports the Israeli government with money and weapons to enable them to carry out this kind of oppression. I live with all of this around me.

I also correspond with a friend who lives in Newark, New Jersey, in one of the worst slums of that huge city. The stories he tells me make the Palestinians' plight almost preferable. Stories of drug overdose, rape, robberies, murders, abandoned children. Then each evening I turn on my shortwave radio to get the mid-East news broadcast from London by the B.B.C. I hear of racial violence in Germany, riots in American cities, ethnic cleansing in Eastern Europe, starvation in Somalia, killings by the hundreds in India over temples and mosques, bombs in Ulster, and the like. What am I to do? These are my brothers and sisters. Not only that, their oppressors are my brothers and sisters. I mean by that the Israeli soldiers, the Newark drug dealers, the Neo Nazis, the Bosnian Army in Yugoslavia, the Somalian gangsters holding back food, the I.R.A. I cannot say "Our Father" without reaching out to all of them and trying to love them. I must do this if I am to pray as Jesus taught me. I also have to help them in some way. What is the will of the Father for me in this regard?

CHAPTER 127

· *Which Speaks of the Will of the Father and Our First Response to the Joys and the Sorrows of Our Brothers and Sisters*

Dear friend, if you have read this far in my little book, you already know one response that you must make. I have already said that we must pray as though everything depended upon God and work as though everything depended upon us. You know how to pray. You know how to enter into the heart of our Father in love and from God's heart to embrace, along with God, all those whom God loves and embraces. You do this by your contemplative meditation.

For some of us, this will be the greatest contribution we can make to our suffering brothers and sisters, and to our other brothers and sisters who cause their sufferings. Others of us recognize a call to contribute by direct action, such as the Maryknollers I spoke about earlier. Still others contribute by financial support, something we can all do, even if it is only by our widow's mite and from our need. All of us can and must act out the meaning of the words "Our Father" in the immediate concrete circumstances of our daily lives. All of us have to respond as well as we can, and as fully as our love will prompt us, to rejoice with the happy and to serve the needy who actually surround us. Again, let me remind you, dear friend, that charity begins at home—but it must not end there. Or, put it this way. With the mass media of communications that we have today, with the outreaching arms, eyes, and ears of newspapers, books, radio, and television, the whole world is a global village. It is brought into our homes daily with all of its delights and tragedies. This must be then the extent of our love.

Be sensitive, dear friend in God, to the promptings of the Holy Spirit, which you will receive as a result of your contemplation. Receive God's consolations and purifications on your personal level but be open and responsive to the ways God will suggest to you for embracing all God's children.

CHAPTER 128

• Which Continues the Our Father to the Second Petition

All of what I have said, dear friend, in the preceding chapters is directly related to the method, the dispositions, and the attitude we must have when we pray as instructed by Jesus. He tells us to pray to a father, to Our Father, and then says, "Who art in heaven." This is very important indeed in what it tells us how it should form our attitude in prayer. Jesus wants us to pray with an understanding that we pray to a *heavenly* father and all that that means.

God is a father, yes, Our Father. It is not impossible that this could be difficult for some people to relate to. What of someone whose idea of *father* is based on brutality received from a father figure in childhood? What of someone who never knew his or her father or whose father abandoned him or her? Jesus is aware of this, dear friend, and this is why he gives us his Father and why he wants us to realize that his Father is a heavenly one. A heavenly Father is not subject to the imperfections of even the best earthly father. Also he sees the whole picture, as it were. He knows us better than we know ourselves.

At the same time, because he is a heavenly Father, "his ways are not our ways, and as far as the heavens are from the earth so far are his ways from our ways" (Isaiah). Because of this, because he is "Our Father who art in heaven," we must expect from him the unexpected. And we must do so with confidence, with faith and with hope.

Scripture scholars tell us that when Jesus told us the parable of the prodigal son, he was actually commenting on the Our Father and trying to tell us just what his heavenly Father was really like. Please to go your Bible and read this parable from chapter 15, verse 11, of St. Luke's Gospel. Let Jesus tell you himself what he means by a heavenly Father (and also what is meant by a real brother or sister)!

CHAPTER 129

• *Which Teaches Us the Third Attitude*
Jesus Tells Us
We Must Have in Prayer

Jesus said, "When you pray, say: 'hallowed be thy name.'" This, dear friend of God, is really the first petition of the Lord's Prayer. Please remember, now as we have been insisting, Jesus wants us to know that his request, "hallowed be thy name" has to have priority in all our prayer. This is his method! The first thing that we should desire is that God be glorified. This is simply an application of the great commandment Jesus taught us. "You shall love the Lord your God with your whole heart, your whole soul, and your whole strength." It only makes sense, does it not, that our greatest desire and first petition be in accord with that command. Thus, in every prayer we offer, this must be our first and overwhelming desire, that God be glorified. All else is subject to that. Any prayer that seeks a priority for any other purpose is idle and vain and "a chasing after the wind." One of the fruits of your contemplative meditation will be a profound understanding of this truth and a desire that in all things God be glorified.

CHAPTER 130

• How the Desire for God's Kingdom in Its Fullness Must Be Prominent in Our Prayer

The next priority, dear friend, that Jesus gives us in our prayer is that we should have a great desire for the coming of God's kingdom. Jesus said, "When you pray, say: 'Thy kingdom come'." Indeed, do you realize that everything we do should have as its ultimate goal the coming of God's kingdom? We must desire what God desires. We must desire and pray and work for a world that will reflect God's will so perfectly that it will be the actual embodiment of God's plan for it—God's kingdom. We must fervently pray: "O Lord, may your kingdom come and may it begin with me."

CHAPTER 131

• How "Thy Kingdom Come" Is Very Often Misunderstood

Dear friend, now that we are approaching the year 2000, we can expect a barrage of truly weird, self-appointed prophets proclaiming the end of the world and the coming of God's kingdom. Indeed, we have already had a plethora of such announcements, giving actual dates for the "Coming" based on foolish misinterpretations of the Bible. As each date passes uneventfully, another is given to take its place. Truly I do not understood what is behind such an attitude. I do not see it as a real desire for the coming of God's kingdom, but as some kind of a collective death wish or a sectarian desire to be proven right and see all who disagree punished by the divine wrath. I do not think such an attitude is in accord with the method of prayer Jesus taught us.

To desire God's kingdom to come is to desire that God's love be freely, fully, and willingly manifested all over the world. You and I, dear friend, have an important job to do in this regard. The love that we have to offer and that God wants to manifest in and through us is essential for the coming of the kingdom. The kingdom of God is, first, within us and, then, manifested in what we do—springing from that love. That is the kingdom of God in power. Earnestly desire it and work for it.

power of healing

CHAPTER 132

· *Which Considers the Dispositions Jesus' Method of Prayer Calls for in the Phrase* Thy Will Be Done on Earth as It Is in Heaven

Dear friend, it is not surprising that we should find Jesus' method of prayer illustrated in his own life as well as taught by his words. The next attitude he tells us we must have in all our prayer is to desire that God's will be done on earth as in heaven. How wonderfully we see this attitude expressed in Jesus' personal life.

I recently spent seven days on a private retreat in the garden of Gethsemane. As you know, this is the place at the foot of the Mount of Olives where Jesus often went to spend the night when he was in Jerusalem. There is a small community of Franciscan Friars there who keep the gardens and staff the beautiful basilica of Gethsemane. They will tell you that many of the ancient olive trees they so carefully tend were growing there when Jesus came to that holy place. I spent many hours of prayer walking through these olive groves and was graced with the opportunity of meditating by the huge rock where the gospel tells us Jesus prayed.

From the garden one looks across the Kidron valley, up the sloping hill of ancient Mount Sion, to the huge stone wall surrounding the Old City of Jerusalem. Gethsemane is directly across the small valley separating the Mount of Olives from the site of the magnificent temple built by King Herod during Jesus' own lifetime. Here, the gospels tell us, Jesus went, after the Last Supper, to pray with his disciples and to await his betrayal by his beloved Judas.

CHAPTER 133

• *Which Offers Us the Prayer of Jesus in Gethsemane as a Model for Our Own Prayer*

We have, dear friend, several examples of Jesus' prayer in the four gospels. None of them, however, are as personal, as intense, as dramatic, and as heart-rending as his prayer in the garden of Gethsemane. He was very much aware of what was to happen in the coming twenty-four hours. His heart was broken, his hopes dashed, his mind reeled with agonized expectation of the physical and mental torments he would have to undergo. With the desperate pleas of a lonely, frightened man, he begged his father to spare him from the horrors he had been led to expect. "Father, if it be possible, let this chalice pass from me!"

It seemed to me, dear friend, as I walked through those olive groves, while the evening breeze gently swayed the drooping branches of the ancient gnarled trees, that I could hear, coming through the dusk-darkened evening surrounding the rock of his agony, his very voice. But it was not the voice of one man. No, it was the millions of voices of my brothers and sisters, each with his or her own litany of sufferings and sorrows, calling out together with Jesus, as his body—the body of Christ—pleading with our heavenly Father to spare them, to relieve them from their agonies.

But then I heard what I can only describe as the "bottom line." I heard the single voice of Jesus speaking in behalf of all of them— of all of us. "But not my will, but thine be done." This is what Jesus shows us must be the ultimate condition or attitude of our every prayer. No matter how personal, how intense, how difficult our situation might be, no matter how great our desire for deliverance, as the "bottom line" we leave it in the hands of our heavenly Father. "Not my will but thine be done." This requires of us, dear friend, great faith, great hope, and great love. But God will be with us through our sufferings, our Good Fridays, our deaths, even to the glory of our Easters. Be assured of this and take comfort in it.

CHAPTER 134

• According to Jesus' Method of Prayer, We Must Also Be Disposed to Ask for Our Daily Bread

We must face a difficulty here, dear friend, as we look at the next disposition Jesus requires of us as he teaches us how to pray. He says, "When you pray, say . . . 'Give us this day, our daily bread'." This seems simple enough. Yet there are some very early manuscripts of the Bible that say here, "Give us this day our supersubstantial bread." In this case, Jesus would clearly have us praying, not for physical, material bread, but for the spiritual bread which is his word and the sacrament of his body and blood.

The real difficulty comes, however, when we read Luke 12:29. "And do not seek what you are to eat and what you are to drink, nor be of anxious mind. For all the nations of the world seek these things; and your Father knows that you need them. Instead seek his kingdom, and these things shall be yours as well." When we look closely at what Jesus is saying, the difficulty resolves itself. In his prayer he speaks of asking for our daily bread with the attitude, as we have seen, that we first are concerned with acknowledging God's holiness ("hallowed be thy name"), seeking his kingdom ("thy kingdom come") and wanting to do his will ("thy will be done"). Then in this context, we may ask for our daily bread. Indeed we should ask for it, and then, of course, work for it as God gives us the means. We should not then be unduly anxious for it, Jesus tells us in the passage from Luke. This is not the same as saying we should not pray for it, or work for it. Please notice, dear friend, that in the passage from St. Luke, Jesus also gives priority to seeking God's kingdom ("Seek his kingdom and these things shall be yours as well"). So I think that we can ask God for anything we wish, as long as it will not be harmful to ourselves or anyone else, and as long as our wish honors the priority of the previous petitions for God's glory, kingdom, and will.

CHAPTER 135
* *In which Jesus Tells Us That We Ourselves Should Place a Condition on the Next Request*

Jesus teaches us that his method of praying calls for us to be forgiving, even as we expect God to forgive us. This is what is so beautifully illustrated in the parable of the prodigal son (Luke 15:11). But did you ever stop to think, dear friend, that if we have even one person in our lives whom we have not forgiven, every time we say the Lord's prayer, we ask our Father not to forgive us! This makes sense, too, in view of what we have said about praying to our Father—that is, in union with Jesus and all our brothers and sisters throughout the world. There is no one our Father has not forgiven if they will simply receive it. So it must be for us.

Our first motivation for forgiving others must be our love for God. Because we wish God's name to be hallowed, his kingdom to come, and God's will to be done, we will forgive our offenders for God's sake. However, we must also do this for our own sake, because we must love ourselves, and for our neighbor's sake, because we must love all others. We do it for our own sake, because God's forgiveness of us is based on our forgiveness of others. Also, and this is most important to understand, when we are unforgiving, it harms *us* personally more than it harms anyone else. For us to refuse forgiveness to anyone is to distort our own God-image. It does us incalculable harm—much more harm than it could possibly do to anybody else. It makes us ugly, unloving, sinful, and something less than human. It is a denial of Christ who said that whatever we do to the least of his brothers, we do to him.

CHAPTER 136

· How There Are Different Levels of Forgiveness

I am sure you realize, dear friend of God, that there are many different levels of forgiveness. As a result of this, forgiveness is something we must constantly be aware of and work on. We have already seen (and, I hope, experienced) that when we pursue in our loving search our contemplative meditation, we enter into the very heart of God. From this place we reach out with God and love all whom God loves—including those who have offended us in any way, in any time of our lives. This is a wonderful, radical, deep-rooted loving and forgiving. But it is not always the whole picture.

Sometimes we also have to work on forgiveness on another level, the emotional level. We have already seen one way to do this in the chapters on compassion meditation. Indeed, one way to know if we have forgiven offenders is our willingness to pray for him or her. Most often we must also work on yet another level. That is the level of reaching out to a former enemy if he or she is alive and if we have not been formally reconciled. Even if he or she will not respond to our outreaching, they must be made to understand that we offer them forgiveness at any time they are willing to accept it. Remember, too, dear friend, that sometimes this means we have to accept an actual injustice they may have performed against us but cannot be made to see it as such. As with God, our mercy must temper our sense of justice. When we place limits on our forgiveness, we ask God to place the same limits on divine forgiveness. "Forgive us our trespasses *as we forgive* those who trespass against us."

CHAPTER 137

• *Which Concludes the Method Jesus Teaches Us*

"Lead us not into temptation but deliver us from evil." Of course, God will not lead us into temptation. This is simply one way of asking for God's help, grace, and strength in the many trials we daily face. It is an acknowledgment of our own weakness and a statement that we are willing to find our strength in God. This is an encouraging and very hopeful attitude. St. Paul tells us (2 Cor. 12:9) that Jesus will make his power "perfect in weakness." So if Paul would recognize his weakness and then depend on Jesus, his very weakness would be his strength. And so St. Paul says, "That is why, for Christ's sake, I delight in weaknesses, in insults, in hardships, in persecutions, in difficulties, for when I am weak then I am strong."

And so, dear friend, we are brought full circle back to the beginning of Jesus' method of prayer. When we admit our weaknesses to our Father who is in heaven, he bends over to take us up in his arms and offer us his strength, his holiness and his love. Thus we do our part to make God's name holy, to bring about the fullness of God's kingdom, and to fulfill God's holy will.

CHAPTER 138

• *Which Finishes This Little Book*

Dear friend, I offer you the advice, the instructions, and the reflections of this little book in a priestly, caring, and loving spirit. Persevere in your loving search for God with humility but also with great desire. Recognize this desire as a wonderful grace in itself and a testimony of God's love for you. Embrace me as I embrace you in the loving prayer of our mutual search. This is a work that we begin here on earth but which we will continue in God's presence forever.

Remember, dear friend, we live in a world that offers much in suffering but also in consolation. You will not always understand it yourself, but seek to love it and seek to love yourself and to be loved. Know that the God of love has created us all, guides us all, and wills to bring us all back to Godself, the source whence we came.

Realize that your efforts to love will always bear fruit even when they seem to have failed; that your compassionate responses will give life to others even when rejected; and that the Holy Spirit of God is the source of all such endeavors. Deal gently with yourself and with others. Judge neither yourself nor others harshly. Correct patiently and receive corrections gratefully. Understand that such give and take and its resulting tensions are signs of life, growth, and maturity. Never cease to grow. Let age bring you wisdom and experience teach you compassion.

Live your love, teach your love, and be your love even as God is love. You are the body of Christ and perhaps, in segments of your world, the only access Christ has. Be Christ then. Let him live and love, give and be received, through you. Allow his love to surround you and emanate from you unhindered by selfishness or pride. I pray that the love God has begun in us, God may continuously call forth from us and bring to a perfect completion. Amen.